EMOTIONAL AND BEHAVIOURAL DIFFICULTIES

John Cornwall

and Janet Tod

£14.25

David Fulton Publishers

London

David Fulton Publishers Ltd
Ormond House, 26–27 Boswell Street, London WC1N 3JZ

www.fultonpublishers.co.uk

First published in Great Britain by David Fulton Publishers 1998
Reprinted 1999, 2000, 2002

Note: The right of John Cornwall and Janet Tod to be identified as the authors of this work
has been asserted by them in accordance with the Copyright, Designs and Patents Act 1988.

Copyright © John Cornwall and Janet Tod 1998

British Library Cataloguing in Publication Data
A catalogue record for this book is available from the British Library

ISBN 1–85346–521–6

Typeset by Textype Typesetters, Cambridge
Printed in Great Britain by Bell and Bain Ltd, Glasgow

Contents

	Principles	**Institutional self-review**	**Ideas for action**
IEPs and EBD	Pages 10 to 17	Pages 18 to 19	Page 20
Assessment and identification	Pages 21 to 26	Pages 27 to 28	Pages 29 to 36
Target setting and strategies	Pages 37 to 41	Page 42	Pages 43 to 52
Coordination and monitoring	Pages 53 to 56	Pages 57 to 59	Pages 60 to 66
Involving the learner	Pages 67 to 77	Pages 78 to 79	Pages 80 to 81
Parental involvement	Pages 82 to 83	Pages 84 to 86	Page 87
Training and continuing professional development	Pages 88 to 90	Page 91	Pages 92 to 100

Acknowledgements

This book results from work undertaken as part of a research project commissioned by the DfEE and managed at the Special Needs Research and Development Centre of the Department of Education of Canterbury Christ Church College of Higher Education.

The authors would like to express their thanks to teachers and officers in the following LEAs who contributed to the project. The views represented in this book are those of the authors and are not intended to represent the views or policies of any particular body or LEA.

Kent Behaviour Support Service
Kent Education Authority
The London Borough of Southwark
The Wirral

In particular, the team would like to acknowledge the contributions from:

Briony Branmer and selected schools in Southwark
Garry Hornby, University of Hull
Robin Howells, Ripplevale School
Keith Humphreys, University of Northumbria
Kate Jacques, St Martin's College, Lancaster
David Moore, HMI
Bonnie Mount, Secretary to the Special Needs Research and Development Centre
Mike Randall, Cathcart Street Primary School, Wirral

How to use this book

Ideas and procedures contained in this book have been developed with practitioners in many different settings. The book is based on observations of current practice and recognises that schools will be at different stages of development and may have differing priorities and resources. The proposed review of the Code of Practice, and the response to the Green Paper on SEN, will be an opportunity for schools to reassess the effectiveness of their procedures in meeting the special educational needs of their pupils.

The format of the book reflects three key aspects of the development of IEP procedures. These are:

Principles

Following the publication of the Code of Practice, many schools focused their efforts upon meeting the Code's administrative requirements for IEPs. Other schools responded to the underlying *principles* and adapted their existing good practice. This allowed them to have regard to the Code while at the same time developing procedures which were manageable given their particular circumstances. For example, the IEP procedure as described in the Code has proven to be particularly challenging for some secondary schools and for schools with a relatively high number of pupils at Stage 2 of the Code and beyond. Each section of this book thus contains a section concerned with principles to be considered by a school in interpreting the Code.

School development via Institutional self-review (ISR)

Effective schools have responded to the demands of the Code in general and IEPs in particular by integrating procedures into their school development planning. This has changed the perception of the Code from that of a set of prescriptions with the emphasis on individual rights and responsibilities into a document which informs and guides an ongoing process of collaborative school development for inclusive SEN provision. Schools are increasingly recognising the need to encourage shared responsibility for IEP procedures. Central to this are the developing roles of parents, pupils and outside agencies. The regular monitoring of the school's collective IEPs has enabled the targeting of resources. Each section of this book contains an *Institutional self-review (ISR)* to enable schools to self-assess and develop their own action plans.

Ideas for action

Many schools have found that class and subject teachers need to be supported in developing skills beyond planning IEP target setting. Some schools are developing their own shared strategy banks, others are using strategies contained in published SENCO support packs as a starting point. A development which is becoming evident in schools is the increasing use of technology (e.g. World Wide Web) for the sharing and exchange of strategies for meeting SEN. One such on-line resource is the SEN Xplanatory (www.canterbury.ac.uk/xplanatory/xplan.htm), developed by Mike Blamires at the Special Needs Research and Development Centre.

Each section of the book contains some *ideas for action* for consideration. For example the section on 'Assessment and identification' seeks to illustrate how IEPs might be integrated into a school's general arrangements for assessment and recording the progress of all pupils. The other sections have been included to address emergent areas of particular relevance to IEP procedures such as 'Target setting', 'Parental involvement', implications for 'Training and continuing professional development' etc.

To use this book, the reader has to select the appropriate section from the grid on the Contents page. This book is intended to provide a practical resource to schools. For example if the SENCO has decided to delegate the setting of targets for IEP planning to class or subject teachers and needs to deliver a staff development activity, the section covering 'Principles of target setting and strategies' will provide a useful starting point.

Individual pupil needs

Reflection	Self-esteem	Anger control	Selective attention	Short-term memory	Turn taking	Sharing	Predicting outcomes of behaviour	Reaction to failure	Self-control	Language

RESOURCES

Whole class

Learning support assistant

SENCO

Parent/ guardian

Pupil

Others, e.g. peers, school counsellor, form tutor, etc.

Outside agencies, e.g. social worker, educational psychologist

This diagram represents the concept of a 'behavioural' IEP. On the right is the curriculum described in key skills – this might be either a subject area or in this case a behavioural curriculum.* This curriculum is shared by all pupils with key skills linked to Key Stages. On the top of the page are descriptors of individual pupil needs. These prescribe the 'different or extra' provision needed to enable the pupil to achieve targeted key skills. On the left hand side are the human resources which can be brought to bear to improve the learning opportunities for the EBD pupil by the application of *coordinated* educational effort (strategies).

KEY SKILLS
- ask for help when needed
- listen and respond
- make choices
- actively participate
- show concern for others' feelings
- try to complete tasks set
- follow class rules
- follow school rules
- be able to forgive others
- help others when appropriate
- understand that own actions affect others – both positively (when saying something nice) and negatively (when criticising or bullying)
- tell the truth
- take responsibility for own actions
- take increasing responsibility for own learning
- recognise and value self and achievements
- have respect for others
- take responsibility for own safety (and health)
- value the friendship of others
- self-direct attention when appropriate
- allow attention to be directed by teacher
- show an interest in other people
- share (experiences, material possessions, attention)
- work cooperatively
- wait turn, turn take
- accept and use criticism
- monitor own work against task instructions
- self-assess own work
- apologise when appropriate
- have respect for property

* It is recognised that there is no national 'behavioural' curriculum and schools may have their own list of desirable skills or feel it useful for staff to agree the 'key skills for learning and social behaviour' appropriate at each Key Stage. QCA (1997) are piloting materials for the development of a Key Stage linked programme to promote pupils' spiritual, moral, social and cultural development.

Figure 1

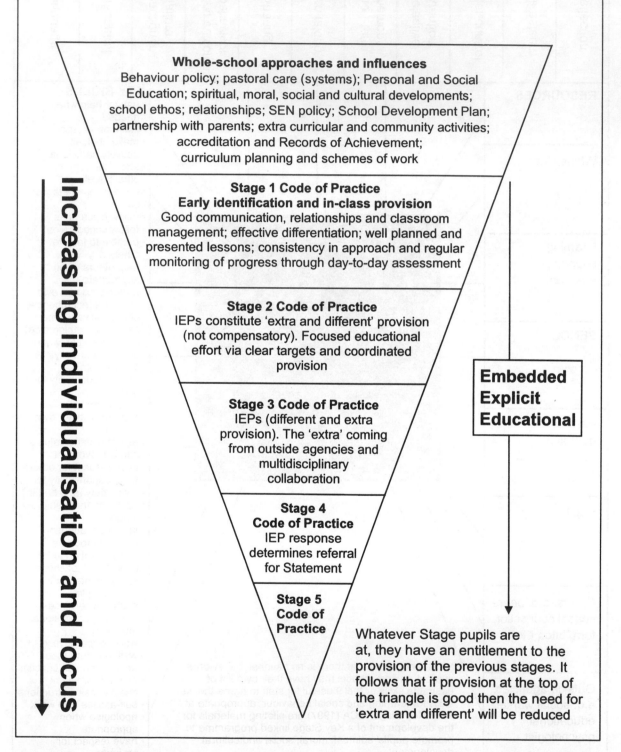

The IEP and the five stages of the Code of Practice

Whole-school approaches and influences
Behaviour policy; pastoral care (systems); Personal and Social Education; spiritual, moral, social and cultural developments; school ethos; relationships; SEN policy; School Development Plan; partnership with parents; extra curricular and community activities; accreditation and Records of Achievement; curriculum planning and schemes of work

Stage 1 Code of Practice
Early identification and in-class provision
Good communication, relationships and classroom management; effective differentiation; well planned and presented lessons; consistency in approach and regular monitoring of progress through day-to-day assessment

Stage 2 Code of Practice
IEPs constitute 'extra and different' provision (not compensatory). Focused educational effort via clear targets and coordinated provision

Stage 3 Code of Practice
IEPs (different and extra provision). The 'extra' coming from outside agencies and multidisciplinary collaboration

Stage 4 Code of Practice
IEP response determines referral for Statement

Stage 5 Code of Practice

Increasing individualisation and focus

Embedded Explicit Educational

Whatever Stage pupils are at, they have an entitlement to the provision of the previous stages. It follows that if provision at the top of the triangle is good then the need for 'extra and different' will be reduced

Figure 2

Introduction: So what's so difficult about 'behavioural' IEPs?

We will start by asking some very basic questions in order to establish some principles upon which to base further Individual Education Plan (IEP) development work. We continue by examining the views, concerns and achievements collectively expressed by many teachers who work with children experiencing Emotional and Behavioural Difficulty (EBD). We then outline some general, but clearly educational, criteria that may help to begin to define the role of teachers in designing and activating 'behavioural' IEPs and finish with some checkpoints for consideration in reviewing your school's approach to pupils who are experiencing EBD.

Some initial questions about IEPs for pupils experiencing EBD

- What is the *purpose* of IEPs generally?

- What is the *purpose of IEPs for 'behaviour'*?

- Is it an accounting activity or genuinely designed to *generate new learning*?

- *Is it educational* (through monitoring and evaluating learning) or administrative?

- Should IEPs exist only to *provide access* to the main curriculum or should they be *part of the whole curriculum*?

- What have they got to do with a pupil's own *longer-term personal development*?

- *What is the role* of the teachers or learning support assistant?

- Does this role include surrogate parenting, counselling or therapy?

- Are IEPs *limited* to individual behavioural targets without due concern for affective or emotional factors?

- Are targets set *within context, and with communication or discussion* as recommended in the Code of Practice?

- Are both *the pupils and parents* being given proper opportunities and encouragement to be *fully involved*?

- Has there been *training to understand the causes* of emotional and behavioural difficulties through individual differences (e.g. self-esteem, learning styles, developmental/age and emotional development)?

- Is the curriculum used effectively to work on broad emotional or behavioural issues without personal confrontation?

In order to begin to consider Individualised Education Planning for pupils experiencing EBD, the views of over 200 teachers and learning support staff, particularly involved with pupils in this category, have been canvassed over a period of four years. Two main questions have been asked:

- What are your main fears and concerns in working with children who experience EBD or show challenging behaviour?

- What have been your main achievements and successes in working with pupils experiencing EBD or showing challenging behaviour?

The following selection of comments clearly illustrates the active engagement of the teacher or adult in being part of the solution. It is in their own words and shows some of the fears and concerns they experience daily.

- Remaining positive.

- Fear of losing control – fear of loss of face.

- Losing control of the class. High noise levels, banging, screaming, shouting.

- Confrontational situations which only result in a no-win situation.

- Being anxious about confrontation with Yr. 5/6. Not knowing if I can cope or will have a successful outcome e.g. dinner queue argument – 'he pushed in' – then, 'no, I didn't'.

- Child who simply refuses to do as asked.

- Failure to deal appropriately with a group or individual.

- Pupil walking out of the room – the sense of failure.

- Losing control of whole class because of dealing with individual.

- Volatile, explosive behaviour. Losing my temper – coming down to their level!

- The contagious effect of bad behaviour (the attempt to lead others in a campaign of disruption; low-key repetitive disruptive behaviour).

- Coping with a child in full-blown temper tantrum who is about to injure himself/herself.

- Losing temper and taking it out on innocent victims. Also being too friendly at times.

- Complete lack of respect for each other, others' property or even their own property.

- The repetitiveness of misbehaviour – they do things time and time again even though they've been told.

- Swearing at staff indiscriminately.

- A child being violent towards me. Would I be able to deal with the situation?

- Aggressive language, physical aggression.

- I find sexual comments very hard to deal with and sexual behaviour.

- I feel anxious about the violence and aggression that some pupils display.

- One pupil overtly bullying another and my impotence in dealing with this. (Even worse – a whole group victimising one individual.)

- Swearing – shows lack of self-respect and respect for others. It angers me – unnecessary and uncivilised.

- Victimisation of one child by group. It becomes so tempting to show them how it feels.

- When a pupil will not work even after many attempts at talking them round.

- Not being able to change 'home' situations where you know the child readily could make it. Getting the child to admit to what you know is the problem from external influences.

- Keeping my cool when they have physically hurt another child.

- Their irrationality.

- Student's lack of insight often makes reasoning and confrontation by teacher impossible. Inappropriate staring by student may cause teacher anxiety.

- I'm worried whether I am doing it right.

So, there is a picture of challenging situations that involves both the adult concerned *and* the pupil. It is an interactive situation, not one that is controlled solely by the behaviour (or so-called 'lack of discipline') of the pupil. Extracting some main themes from the above list enables us to identify some of the reasons why IEPs for pupils experiencing EBD are different.

The actual behaviour is influenced by internal factors in the pupils and internal factors in the adult, as well as a whole array of external factors. To talk about changing behaviour alone is too simple a solution. To expect there to be discrete remedies, instant solutions or even quick treatments is storing up further problems, if not for the school, certainly for society in the long term. From teachers' comments it would appear that 'behavioural' IEPs create particular problems because:

- situations regularly *challenge the competencies and knowledge* of the adults involved;

- *personal relationships cause problems* and the skills to handle these effectively are not always to hand;

- *classroom management and group dynamics* often provide a challenge, particularly to less experienced teachers (though not exclusively);

- *there is fear involved* – fear of losing control, of taking action that damages their professional standing or of the consequences of failure to themselves and to their pupils.

Teachers and other adults who work directly with children experiencing EBD

If we now look at teachers commenting on their successes and achievements:

- Having positive remarks made by the 'public' about the boys i.e. well behaved, worked hard etc. (during work experience etc.).

- Taught a girl a technique to use when she felt she was losing her temper, so she wouldn't start fighting – it worked.

- Getting the boys to turn up to PE lessons and get changed into kit.

- Stopping a percentage of pupils from physically abusing me.

- Boy in tantrum and being very stressed – been able to talk and calm down the boy.

- Getting pupils to talk about problems instead of shouting and using bad language. Cutting down bad language in general.

- Make sure the children stay in class because they want to, not because I've made them.

- To be able to talk and listen with a calming influence. Boy 1: settles down at bedtime; Boy 2: realises he is swearing and tries to improve; Boy 3: able to sit at the meal table and eat properly.

- My discovery that I could address and even hold the attention of large groups and even the whole school. The atmosphere can occasionally become relevant and even electric.

- Being the first teacher to have an impact on a child's behaviour to the extent that on reintegration to mainstream he is still doing well a year on.

- Telling a pupil he/she is wrong for having a go at other pupils. To have forgotten about the incident and then to find the pupil turns up to say 'YES, you are right'.

- When our school 'bully' served a meal to the teachers at a French event and so enjoyed it that we ended up writing to catering colleges to keep up his enthusiasm. He made it!

- Working with a dyspraxic child whom I got involved in football.

- Turning a very reluctant reader onto reading – one day he wouldn't stop reading. Quote – 'It's your fault. You got me into reading!'

- I consider achievement to be the result of a team effort, rather than 'my' achievement. One such success, which I found very exciting, was maintaining eye contact for the first time with a particularly aggressive student, known for her lack of eye contact.

- The child was able to sit on the mat and listen to a story all the way through without comments.

- Past pupil returns after two years and gives hug and thanks for putting him 'on right track'.

- Weekly and daily tick and star charts for acceptable behaviour. Also own targets set weekly which are achievable. Noticeable difference with autistic child.

- I was able to allow a child to work through his temper, disobedience, tantrum, tears etc. until calm was restored and we emerged (eventually) with a wonderful relationship.

- To find a way through to a child enabling manageable behaviour.

- Pupil who returned to school full time after a period of refusing completely.

- Raising the self-esteem of a dyslexic child. He was voted best dancer by the school and success built on success. Getting a Yr. 7 child repeating his Yr. 6 to believe he could do sums. Getting a child to sit still long enough to learn. Went from reading one word at beginning of year to Level 2 SATs at end.

- Enabling teenage mothers to access curriculum, both academic and personal.

- Child learned not to take 'justice' revenge into his own hands – but began to refer situation to adult.

- Eighteen-year-old coming to see me. In work, living with someone in a flat with his two children and at work. A reasonable human being.

- Having a class so settled that its dynamics can change intrusive behaviour.

- Meeting one of my ex-pupils who had quite severe behaviour problems. He was a well adjusted, happy, settled adult with a good career.

We can see that they feel positive about:

- achieving some of the *required goals for learning*;

- *meeting the needs of their pupils and developing good relationships* in the classroom;

- gaining an element of *control of the learning environment*;

- being able to *recognise when learning or progress has taken place*;

- enjoying personal satisfaction when *positive changes are recognised*.

Clearly, there are gains for both pupils and teachers when effective planning enables progress to be achieved and recognised. The IEP process should be integral to meeting individual needs, nurturing professional development and supporting whole-school development. Teachers report that IEPs have:

- provided a vehicle for the development of collaboration and involvement with parents and a mechanism for enabling pupils to become more involved in their own learning plans;

- directed teacher attention towards the setting and resetting of clear educationally relevant targets;

- involved all staff in the development and implementation of strategies to meet those targets;

- harnessed available material and human resources to meet those strategies through focused and coordinated 'educational' effort;

- increased the emphasis on monitoring and evaluating pupils' responses to teaching in terms of progress;

- provided clearer evidence as to the effectiveness of additional SEN provision.

This book promotes a broad but educational viewpoint which is summarised below. It is the *teacher's responsibility* to promote:

- good relationships;

- a secure and positive atmosphere in the classroom;

- an efficiently organised learning environment.

This can be *achieved through*:

- careful planning;

- an understanding and problem-solving approach;

- skilful presentation and organisation of planned activities.

Delivering the curriculum effectively usually means:

- fostering good relationships with pupils;

- encouraging good relationships between pupils in collaborative tasks.

The complexity of *classroom management* means that teachers need to show a skilled approach to:

- groups and their dynamics;

- presenting learning materials sensitively;

- having high expectations but with due regard for individual abilities.

Teachers and learning or special support staff are constantly *developing their teaching skills* to:

- recognise when learning, progress or changes in behaviour have been established;

- clearly identify progress against curricular and individualised targets;

- recognise and accept individual differences within the overall curriculum.

Teachers' professional training, the requirements of the curriculum and time allocation make it difficult for them to act as surrogate parents, counsellors, practising psychologists, foster parents, policemen, sex therapists or all the other roles that might be expected of them. The professional skills of a teacher include an awareness of the role of the IEP in establishing where progress is not occurring and the collaborative skills to engage other colleagues and professionals where appropriate. Teachers have reported particular difficulties associated with developing and using IEPs for pupils experiencing EBD and it seems there are more complications involved, on a broader front, than with other forms of learning difficulty.

Why are IEPs for pupils experiencing EBD apparently so different from other areas of SEN?

This may be due to the fact that teachers see 'behaviour' and 'emotion' as peripheral to 'learning' and the 'curriculum'. Interestingly, Bate and Moss 1997 found that 'each key stage teacher expects children to have learned behavioural skills before they enter the Key Stage which they teach' (p. 177). Teachers may feel that coping with emotion and behaviour is outside their professional competence and thus they feel unnecessarily insecure. As a consequence, there has been a tendency for behavioural IEPs to risk becoming:

- individual, separate and isolated, concerned solely with deficits within the child;

- exclusive and separated from usual practice;

- static and not the trigger for a dynamic process.

When these occur, teachers find themselves with additional tasks with which they may not feel secure and which often do not result in progress towards meaningful objectives.

Another reason why teachers find 'behavioural' IEPs particularly challenging is that they may be well designed and logical but only work in the short term. Characteristically, children with EBD bring to school with them behaviour which is essentially 'adaptive'. That is, they have responded to their environment by actively making sense of their experiences and protecting themselves from further failure or hurt. This 'adaptive' behaviour may have been built up over years and the timing of the short-term IEP (termly) is insufficient to change this 'long-term behaviour'. To change adaptive behaviour is challenging for the teacher and disturbing for the child, and teachers have to 'weather' the inevitable vagaries in pupil behaviour as they gradually move towards targets. It is important that teachers recognise that apparent setbacks and lapses in behaviour are an integral part of the child's struggle to adapt to his changing environment. It is important for the teacher to retain a longer-term vision of progress in the face of these setbacks and not become too personally absorbed in each failure.

Often the effectiveness of a 'behavioural' IEP is dependent on achieving consistency across a range of situations, some of which are beyond the teacher's control. For example, an IEP may be effective in enhancing a pupil's confidence in the classroom only to have it undermined by a parent unwittingly making negative comparisons with a sibling. Sometimes, outside influences like this will have a greater impact upon the pupil than in-school experiences, particularly given that pupils spend more time out of school than in school. It is sometimes necessary for teachers to acknowledge that in-school progress does make a difference for the pupil even when targets are not fully met and have to be adjusted. It is important that teachers maintain a sense of perspective and set themselves realistic targets which enable them to gain some satisfaction from their considerable efforts.

The Code of Practice prescribes a 'staged' model for the identification and provision for Special Educational Needs (SEN). As teachers know, many EBD pupils do not typically exhibit mild behavioural difficulties before proceeding at a measured pace towards greater need for support. For some children, the build up of emotion can trigger an outburst of extreme behaviour which requires the involvement of outside agencies and may result in exclusion. Effectively, these pupils have moved straight to Stages 3, 4 and 5 without experiencing Stage 1 or 2. Although EBD is recognised as a category of need within the Code of Practice at paragraph 3:64, p. 58, the procedures described do not always sit comfortably with the reality experienced by teachers.

Schools are often harsh, overcrowded, noisy and competitive environments, sometimes even cruel, in which children have to adapt and survive. The exclusion of increasing numbers of children from schools and the vilification of pupils who find it hard to access the curriculum because of their emotional and behavioural difficulties is not acceptable. There have to be adjustments and adaptations to the system, including IEPs, as well as the clear definition of an educational approach and the limits of a teacher's responsibilities.

This book supports a positive approach to teaching and classroom management skills and whole-school development. It encompasses an educational approach to helping pupils who are experiencing EBD, and to advancing their learning and academic progress through the use of IEPs and within a progressive and structured curriculum or longer-term plan for personal development.

To summarise, we recognise that there are particular difficulties with IEPs concerned with the emotional and behavioural domain. However, the Code of Practice clearly states:

Pupils with emotional and/or behavioural difficulties have *learning* difficulties ... (authors' italics)

(Code of Practice, 3:64, p. 58)

Teachers are skilled and trained to promote learning, and learning is what is required for behaviour to change. The IEP is an educational tool that can have a powerful impact on a pupil's progress. Much has been achieved as a consequence of the gains that schools have made to coordinate educational efforts in getting IEPs up and running. However, to date, the static and often cumbersome written Plan has overshadowed the need to develop a manageable and focused Process. It would be unfortunate if, after three years of dynamic and collaborative development activity, the administrative burden of IEPs was allowed to occlude the benefits of applying the educational *principles* inherent in the philosophy of IEPs. This book seeks to build on the progress that your school has made so far by placing an emphasis on monitoring and evaluation aspects of IEPs. It does this by focusing attention upon the benefits to pupils in terms of their educational progress.

Discussion points for institutional self-review

This checklist might provide an opportunity to consider some basic principles with regard to your school's whole approach to IEPs and to EBD.

	Teachers	Learning or special support staff	SENCO and school management team
What is the *purpose* of IEPs generally?			
What is the *purpose of IEPs for 'behaviour'*?			
Is it an accounting activity or genuinely designed to *generate new learning*?			
Is it educational (through monitoring and evaluating learning) or administrative?			
Should IEPs exist only to *provide access* to the main curriculum or should they be *part of the whole curriculum*?			
What have they got to do with a pupil's own *longer-term personal development*?			
What is the role of the teachers or learning support assistant?			
Does this role include surrogate parenting, counselling or therapy?			
Are IEPs *limited* to individual behavioural targets without due concern for effective or emotional factors?			
Are targets set *within context, and with communication or discussion* as recommended in the Code of Practice?			
Are both *the pupils and parents* being given proper opportunities and encouragement to be *fully involved*?			
Has there been *training to understand the causes* of emotional and behavioural difficulties?			

IEPs and EBD: Principles

Summary

- The purpose of IEPs is to enable the child to make progress – not to change the child to fit the system.

- Teachers are experts in learning and *can* implement effective behavioural IEPs.

- Teachers cannot be expected to perform multiprofessional functions (e.g. therapy, counselling, parenting, social work, psychiatric support etc.) and should know how and when to refer pupils for outside help.

- Teachers need to be aware that they have an effect on a pupil's emotional state and that this, in turn, affects pupil learning. This is particularly true for anxious children.

- IEPs need to be explicit, embedded and educational; not complex, isolated and administrative.

- IEPs are most effective when they promote the active involvement of pupil and parents in the learning process.

- The effectiveness of an IEP should not be judged by the written Individual Education *Plan* but by the effect it has on a pupil's progress.

- Monitoring pupil response to the IEP is a key area for development in schools.

- IEPs have been a successful vehicle for addressing diversity and involving all staff in SEN provision. The strength of the IEP lies in its effect on planning. It should not be abandoned simply because it is time-consuming and cumbersome, rather it should be streamlined to be more efficient.

IEPs: individual or remedial?

An individual or remedial type model of implementing IEPs expects the problem to reside solely within the child and the 'remedy' to be situated there too. There is the implication that:

- the only thing that needs to change is something 'within the child';

- once the 'treatment' or intervention is completed, everything will revert to normal – there is *little regard for broader evaluation or maintenance*;

- the remedy *relies solely on the expertise of others* outside the classroom and sometimes outside the school;

- *implementation causes problems for all* – of availability, timetabling and equality of opportunity for the pupil;

- *the pupil may be stigmatised* by having to have special treatment or education with its attendant discomfort and sometimes social ridicule;

- it may also become narrow in its focus *and not be related to the broader needs of the pupil* both in school and beyond school *or the teacher(s)*;

- it may relate solely to limited skills useful only in the classroom or in a specific setting and *cannot be usefully generalised to broader situations*;

- it is related to particular ideologies and *treatments promoted by those with vested interests* inside or outside the school;

- the programme will not necessarily be evaluated in terms of long-term benefits to the pupil and leaves you with *the problem of 'where to go from here'* once the limited targets have been achieved.

At the end of the day, all of the pressure is on the pupil to change, to achieve and to conform with little recognition of the fact that change is a contract with the context and surroundings, including others in that environment.

> If you genuinely want someone else to change their behaviour, you have to change your own behaviour in some way first.

This is of particular importance for pupils with EBD in that traditional IEPs for them contain such targets as 'increased time on task', 'attend regularly' – i.e. something wrong with the child, rather than strategies and curricular activities that will enable the pupil to take part in the learning process. There is a tendency to adopt a behavioural disciplinary model rather than a curricular and learning model. These provide short-term and environment-specific behavioural changes without dealing with the broader learning and social behaviours. It is at odds with the OFSTED criteria in *Pupils' personal development and behaviour* (Framework 1995a, Part 1, Section 5, p. 21) and *Attitudes, behaviour and personal development* (The OFSTED Handbook 10/95 1995b, Section 4.2, p. 60).

An IEP drawn up in this mould will be characterised by individual behavioural expectations, treatments, therapies, perhaps medication of some sort. It may segregate and marginalise pupils as being different and requiring 'special' approaches removed from the context of general education. Many teachers and educators understand that learners are diverse in their needs and capabilities and that this very diversity enriches education and its practices. IEPs should be *embedded* in what is happening generally in the school – that is, the ethos, policy, guidance, schemes of work, planning of teaching, support for learning and evaluating success to inform future planning. Eliminating disruption and disaffection completely is not realistic (Elton 1987). There will always be a small number (probably between 5 and 10 per cent) of pupils who will create substantial problems in schools because of the degree to which they do not respond to a carefully planned and sensitive approach. Ensuring good quality class or subject teaching and good quality relationships in the school generally are the most important ingredients for success with the majority of pupils in mainstream schools experiencing EBD. This will then have the effect of highlighting the real problems that exist for that small number of pupils and enable a school to deal with them more effectively. A fragmented approach masks children's real problems . . .

Teachers at the Ridings School, Ovenden, Halifax, have threatened to strike unless action is taken against 60 pupils. The teachers have identified the pupils as trouble makers and want to see them disciplined or expelled. Staff morale at the school is so low that the Headteacher and her deputy have resigned, exhausted by their battle to keep order.

(*Hull Daily Mail* 22 October 1996)

Or do you opt for more of *a social and educational model* that encompasses the relationship between the learner and his or her environment? In this model the IEP will be equally concerned with how:

... the particular needs of individual pupils and groups of pupils ... are met within the teaching and the life of the school generally.

(OFSTED Framework 1995a)

It is encapsulated in the OFSTED criteria in *Pupils' personal development and behaviour* and *Attitudes, behaviour and personal development* referred to a little earlier. These criteria support the notion that the quality of teaching, the long-term personal development of the pupil and the quality of relationships in a school are fundamental to developing positive learning attitudes in pupils. Some extracts illustrate this notion of positive attitudes for learning by looking at how pupils show that they, for example:

- are well motivated, interested and responsive;
- attempt to listen, sustain concentration and persevere with their work;
- respond to challenges, show initiative and take responsibility;
- ask and answer questions;
- contribute to discussion;
- confidently generate ideas in various forms or media;
- solve problems that are appropriately focused to their understanding;
- share their work with others as well as working independently;
- select and use relevant resources;
- review their work and improve it by setting targets for themselves.

A number of good things have emerged from the 1993 Education Act and its subsequent Code of Practice. It has:

- generated IEPs from the Code of Practice. This has helped to *create a new focus on individual differences in learning*. This was done with the intention of giving more detailed guidance to teachers in mainstream schools about learners who are experiencing EBD;
- provided a *vehicle for collaborative work* with parents and pupils;
- involved staff in the development of strategies to meet IEP targets and therefore *increased communication between staff and subject departments*;

- placed an emphasis on the need to be *clear about intentions in teaching* and in learning outcomes;

- highlighted the need for *a match between planning and resources* needed to meet diverse needs and abilities;

- developed *a professional role for SENCOs* and given some status to their activities within mainstream schools.

In looking at more than four years of application that has followed the Code of Practice, it is clear that, despite the many positive effects it had, there are also some less helpful aspects of its implementation, coupled with some misinterpretations. There is also the problem of confusion between Statutory Orders and guidance in education. Some schools are trying to follow the spirit of the 1993 Education Act and others are following the 'letter of the law', sometimes to the detriment of their own best practice.

IEPs: standards and inclusion

Are current IEPs raising standards and are they inclusive? There are several questions about the whole process of developing and implementing IEPs that need to be considered before we get into the mechanics of how it can be done.

- What is the general purpose of IEPs?

- Who do they serve and what is going to be achieved by a time-consuming and sometimes complex process?

There has been a debate about whether the term *Individual Education Plan* should not really be *Individualised Education Plan* simply because the plan should not be totally individual and divorced from the educational opportunity that is given to other pupils. By doing this we avoid having to answer three further awkward questions about the motives of the school:

- Are we intent on 'singling out' individuals and putting them apart from others because the narrow competitive nature of attainment in education won't account for their progress?

- Or are we simply satisfying a need to be 'accountable' by constructing a new framework especially for 'different' groups', thereby enhancing and underlining their separateness from the main thrust of educational policy and teaching?

- Are we implying that some pupils cannot gain access to and be included in the shared curriculum of mainstream children, thereby disclaiming their entitlement?

If we are, then we are setting up further problems in education and beyond education in our schools, communities and cities. The currently increasing number of excluded children (Parsons *et al*. 1997) already indicates that many children are not successfully accessing the curriculum being offered. We are creating an educational underclass who will become increasingly disaffected and often disruptive and whose opportunities to become contributing members of society will be diminished.

We now have the 1997 Green Paper *Excellence for All Children: Meeting Special Educational Needs* which emphasises raising standards for all, including pupils with special needs through inclusive educational practice and working collaboratively with outside agencies. More specifically, it outlines the following areas for action:

- *Policies for excellence* – for *all* children, including those with SEN, through target setting, new technology and improving the standards of literacy and numeracy

- *Working with parents* – to give real opportunities to influence and contribute, while reducing the exceptional pressures they face, through partnership with LEAs and voluntary bodies

- *Practical support: the framework for SEN provision* – reducing wasteful procedures and paperwork with less emphasis on the need for statements

- *Increasing inclusion* – the level and quality in mainstream while protecting and enhancing specialist provision

- *Planning SEN provision* – planning support in both mainstream and specialist facilities, whether maintained, voluntary or private

- *Developing skills for teachers and others* – to make reality of the proposal for inclusion and raising standards for all children

- *Working together* – means effective multi-agency cooperation and contribution to raise standards, use resources more appropriately and to give practical support to increasing inclusion

- *Emotional and behavioural difficulties* – the increasing number of children who provide special challenges need early identification to prevent underachievement, disaffection and often exclusion.

Aside from setting out a basic philosophical 'stall' to drive and rationalise an approach to EBD generally, the challenge for the book is to examine issues, suggest development for schools, and also to highlight strategies for raising standards and including pupils and students identified as experiencing EBD. In other words, let's make them into 'Green' and 'Inclusive' IEPs, rather than IEPs that create a separate world for a child and do not allow for long-term social development and acceptance. This is an equal opportunity standpoint and will tend to be more inclusive, characterised by adjustments to policies, management and arrangements both in the class and in the school generally. It will be concerned with the whole process of teaching and learning as an issue of access to the whole curriculum, not to modifying or manipulating behaviour in a very narrow context.

While schools have tackled the design of formats and the application of IEPs, there is now a need to further develop effective procedures for monitoring and evaluation of the *educational* value for individual pupils. There is little doubt that documentation is largely in place but procedures to review and ensure that progress is taking place for individuals are still very much in development. Procedures to make these static accountability documents into active educational planning is still hampered by a number of factors:

- *lack of planning time* allocated by the roles and conditions of teaching and by individuals themselves;

- *inefficient allocation and non-acceptance of roles* and responsibilities by all staff, but also by pupils and parents requiring strong management support and sensitive promotion;

	Disciplinary or pastoral	Academic and learning
Code of Practice	Tendency to become separatist and exclusive. For example, some schools were far too ready to exclude pupils; others did so with great reluctance, often at some cost to staff and other pupils (Exclusions from Secondary Schools 1995/6, published by OFSTED).	Remedial and 'add on' due to the reviving of 'special' categories which children do not ever completely fit. Good framework for assessment and provides clear indicators of conditions for access to and progress in the curriculum.
Green Paper	Attempting to be more social and inclusive by promoting policies for excellence for all, working with parents (not new), reducing wasteful paperwork, more effective collaboration and *early identification of EBD*.	Curricular and linked to progress by improving mainstream inclusion, planning further support for SEN provision and further developing skills for teachers in classroom management, early identification and developmental approaches.
'Individualised' Planning (IEPs)	Encourages better comparison with group norms and shared rules.	Bridges the potential gap between an individual curriculum and the shared curriculum – avoids removal of pupil's entitlement to a broad and balanced curriculum – no matter what the problem might be.
'Individual' Planning (IEPs)	Tendency to focus on individual deficiencies or weaknesses, particularly in behaviour.	Contains the dilemma of reintegrating back into a shared curriculum, even when an individual curriculum has readjusted some of the difficulties.

- there has been a tendency to *regard the IEP as a separate SEN activity* coordinated by the SENCO when in fact it should be integrated into ongoing curricular planning;

- *sheer amount of paperwork* resulting from a tendency for practitioners and LEAs to interpret the detail as mandatory rather than have regard to the educational principles involved;

- recognition that an IEP is a planning document *informed from the child's educational needs and pupil's progress*, not an evidence base of the school's overall response to justify resource allocation;

- *the interpretation of the term 'individual'* for IEPs has resulted in an emphasis on identification, remediation and treatment of specific categories of disorder rather than a flexible mechanism for deriving both individualised targets for pupils as well as creative strategies for teachers;

- in secondary schools where departments are somewhat separate and autonomous, there are *difficulties of communication and consistency* across the school, not so prevalent in primary schools.

IEPs have not been as successful for pupils with EBD as they have with other forms of learning difficulty. This is partly because the model promoted has not acknowledged the interactive and 'process' nature of working with pupils who are disaffected or disruptive. It is also unable to account for the rapidly changing circumstances involved and the rapidly changing peaks and troughs in progress or attainment, whether academic or personal in nature.

Can school intervention and IEPs make a difference or are the problems too large and external to the classroom to enable change to take place? Should it be limited to raising standards, and inclusion be considered only as a long-term goal through academic success? If the 'standards' are only referenced against external criteria, such as GCSE and SATs results, then it is difficult to reconcile the two key themes of the Green Paper, namely raising standards *and* including pupils. Pupils experiencing emotional and behavioural difficulties are, by definition, directly affected by many more external (i.e. outside school) factors than most other types of specially labelled children. Figure 3 (from McGuiness 1993) illustrates some of the many factors that come to bear upon the emotional and behavioural difficulties experienced by any one child.

> Schools do not work in a vacuum, nor do staff work in a climate unaffected by the larger, different worlds within which we and our pupils live.
>
> (McGuiness 1993)

It is important to be clear about the source of disaffection, disruption or incidents that cause problems for the school or an individual teacher. There may be factors inherent in the way the school is run or there may be events in a pupil's life at school, such as bullying or harassment, that contribute to disaffected or disruptive behaviour. John McGuiness calls it the 'pathogenic influence of school' itself. The influence of things outside the school such as the requirement to follow the National Curriculum, other government legislation or the effect of family life on a child, are deemed the *Sociogenic effect*. In any situation where specific incidents of behaviour are unacceptable, inappropriate or causing major problems for a school, it is important to consider the factors that:

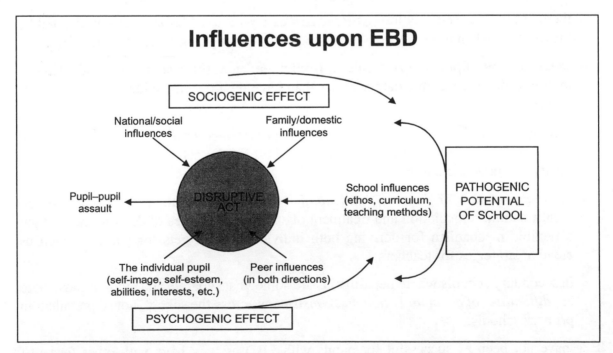

Figure 3

- teachers can influence directly;

- require a whole-school approach;

- require support from outside the school;

- are determined completely outside schools altogether.

This has important ramifications for the development and use of IEPs in behaviour. It is tempting to believe that teachers can have no influence upon behaviour that emanates from sources outside the school. This is not so. Carefully planned IEPs and sensitively executed intervention in a classroom may not change the world outside much but may have considerable impact upon an individual pupil. Many teachers have expressed frustration because they identify the sources of some behaviour as emanating from media 'role models' or stereotyped aggressive behaviour in films. The final area for consideration is the *Psychogenic effect*. This means the factors that are within the children, or are immediately impacting on the way they function in school or the way they see themselves generally. You could say that these are also affected by family life and by the school, but for the purposes of problem solving effectively through the formulation of an IEP, we need to separate out various effects and influences and their sources as the first step.

Whole-school approaches – why? We must not forget then that *teachers and other adults who work directly with children experiencing EBD are a major part of the solution to their difficulties.* The interactive and transactional nature of these types of problem means that *relationships* are fundamental.

IEPs are aimed at improving pupils' attainments in the curriculum – they are an *educational* plan, *not* an Individual Care or Therapy Plan. The school is not a particularly therapeutic environment and schooling is not a therapeutic medium. That is not to say that learning is not therapeutic and there are many approaches such as *Behaviour Therapy* and *Cognitive Therapy* where aspects of changing behaviour and thinking can have an overall therapeutic effect. This is, though, a far cry from the average primary or secondary school environment where school politics, constraints on time and resources, work circumstances or the social environment often militate against teachers' and other adults' attempts to adopt a therapeutic approach to pupils in difficulty.

IEPs are successful when they promote effective planning by teachers and assist pupils to make progress through the setting and reviewing of particular *learning* targets. (authors' italics)

(OFSTED 1996/97)

IEPs and EBD: Institutional self-review

Place your IEPs on firm foundations

Have you had the opportunity to audit or review the basic requirements of the Code of Practice in your school? Use a scale of 1–7 to rate your school or service in relation to these areas outlined below. You can use the comments column to record why you have given it a high (or low) mark and perhaps discuss with colleagues to see how much you agree.

Code of Practice	Your rating	Comments (e.g. why that score?)
Does the school have working policies on pastoral care and guidance and *does it follow them?*		
Are staff fully informed about the school or unit's approach to discipline and is *behaviour managed consistently* across the staff?		
Are there *constructive relationships* surrounding the pupil with EBD and does this include the *involvement of parents or carers*?		
Has *external advice* been sought in developing a meaningful programme for the individual pupil and is this external advice *reflected in the pupil's IEP* or individual programme?		
Has a proactive approach been adopted involving the EWO or Social Service departments *in advance of crisis points whenever possible*?		
Is Information Technology (IT) *used effectively to stimulate and motivate* pupils who find it hard to concentrate and participate?		
When appropriate, has assistance been sought from medical sources (e.g. from Doctor or GP with parental consent)?		

Compare your IEPs with the characteristics below and consider any possible adjustments.

- It is rooted within the planning for all pupils within the class.

- It is positive in tone and pays due recognition to pupil strengths.

- It is social in context.

- It triggers a dynamic response to individual needs.

- It describes the 'extra and different' provision needed by the pupil in relation to provision made at Stage 1 of the Code of Practice. That is, it is not 'instead of' but *additional to*'. Clearly it follows that if provision at whole-school level and at Stage 1 is effective, the need for 'extra and different' is likely to be reduced.

- It seeks to harness available human and physical resources such that 'educational effort' is *coordinated and focused* towards the attainment of relevant and achievable targets.

- It is linked to the curriculum.

- It is comprehensible and can be implemented by those involved.

- It can be regularly monitored, evaluated and adjusted accordingly.

- It is based on an assessment of pupil progress.

- It seeks to move the pupil from 'what he can do' to 'what is expected'. Short-term target setting is linked to medium-and long-term objectives.

- Integral to planning is the acknowledgement that 'new' behaviours need to be consolidated and generalised.

- It reflects the active involvement of pupil and parent (guardian/carer).

IEPs and EBD: Ideas for action

Child not attending to the task or lesson

Look at the following behaviours, discuss with colleagues as appropriate and either tick ✓ or make comment in the appropriate boxes.

	Biolog-ical	Social	Psycholog-ical	Can't do – hasn't developed the behaviour	Won't do – has decided not to	Implications for target setting
Has not grasped the unspoken conventions of the classroom						
Possible underlying condition (e.g. ADD, Tourette's syndrome)						
Lacks early experiences needed to promote attention skills (shared attention, adult-directed and self-directed attention)						
Has not reached the stage of development needed to self-monitor						
Peers expect this kind of behaviour						
As a consequence of previous failure, pupil feels he cannot achieve and there's no point in attending						
Attentional space is taken up with anxiety (biological or social) or with more basic needs (food, sleep) (biological)						
Doesn't understand the language of the curriculum						
Gets more attention from not attending than from attending						

Assessment and identification

What sort of pupils need a behavioural IEP?

Prior to school entry, children 'learn to behave' in particular ways in response to their environment. Once in school, pupils have to 'behave to learn' and for some pupils this is not an easy transition. Interestingly, parents and/or carers recognise that the school environment places different behavioural demands on children than that expected in the home and seek to prepare their children for this transition. Early on in their child's life, the emphasis is on communicating with their infant by seeking to establish 'joint attention'. Parents follow their infant's line of gaze and comment on the object of interest. This facilitates the development of joint attention and language so necessary for effective communication. This period of child-led activity and 'unconditional regard' lays the foundation for the development of self-esteem and in addition ensures that the child is successful in gaining adult attention. A child who is secure in their ability to gain attention does not continually seek it and indeed is more likely to cope with the parental separation experienced on entry to school.

Once their infant has developed language, parents skilfully begin to change their communication style at times so as to prepare their child for school. Instead of merely communicating socially, the adult adopts a 'teaching style' approach and asks the child questions such as 'what colour are your shoes?' – 'how many plates do we need to put on the table?' Similarly, they move from seeking to establish 'joint attention' to developing in their child the skill of having their attention directed by an adult: 'Let's make a nice picture to put on the fridge' – 'Find the red pencil and draw me a lovely apple.' They also try to get their child to sit down, listen, and engage in school-type activities – reading, drawing, number etc. Parents can often offer the one-to-one attention needed for the initial development of this 'on task' behaviour. They encourage their child to make choices and to direct his/her own attention. 'What would you like to draw? Think about what colour you would like the roof to be. Can you be very clever and finish off the picture by yourself?' Feedback is often given so that the child can get used to being corrected and become aware of 'conventions' – 'Do you think the roof looks nice blue? Houses don't have blue roofs do they? I think you are being silly – why don't you colour it brown like our roof?'

Similar strategies are applied to enable their child to develop social skills needed for school. Their child is encouraged to play with same-age peers and social behaviours such as listening, turn taking, sharing etc. are made explicit and rewarded: 'Here's some sweets – give one to Martyn and one to Peter – good boy for sharing'. These behaviours are developed in a supportive safe setting for the child so that the chances of success are maximised. The important point to note is that these behaviours are explicitly taught and *learned* during the years prior to school entry. If a child does not have these experiences, and arrives in school without the appropriate 'learning behaviours', then he/she will not only make slower academic progress and have more peer-related problems but will have to acquire these behaviours in a group setting where failure is public. For some children this 'developmental delay and/or impairment' can be addressed in school by using an available adult and selected peers to recreate home-type situations as described above so that necessary behaviours can be developed initially in a safe setting. Children seek to *make sense of their environment and protect themselves from further failure and rejection.* To do this they develop particular ways of thinking and behaving, e.g.:

- If not given sufficient attention from a parent during the early years, they may constantly seek attention even if it results in an uncomfortable experience e.g. being shouted at or smacked.

- If they are not allowed to succeed, they may decide not to attempt to do anything in case they fail.

- They may adopt a style of thinking e.g. '*everyone* hates me' to protect themselves from rejection and then behave in such a way as to confirm that their belief is correct.

- They may believe that they are the cause of events (e.g. they caused their parents to split up, they are too 'thick' to be able to do school work). If they believe that they cannot change events, then they stop trying to change but carry with them the burden of guilt and failure.

In essence, the 'EBD' pupil may simply not have the appropriate behaviours in their repertoire, in which case some behavioural approaches aimed to build up and reward new skills may be very appropriate and successful. However, if the individual concerned has made an active 'adjustment' to his individual circumstances and the consequent behaviour serves a purpose, then simply trying to change that behaviour without reference to the function will not achieve the desired result. As a simple example, a child who chats with peers in order to avoid starting work (so that he cannot 'fail') could be 'stopped' from chatting. However, the fact that he had stopped would not enable him to lose his fear of failure. He would then develop another behaviour which serves to protect him from revealing his difficulty with his work. Teachers need to be able to decide whether the pupil 'can't' or 'won't' behave and adjust strategies accordingly:

- It is necessary to *ask,* 'are we trying to change this pupil to "fit the school"?'

- It is often necessary to *realise* that the pupil is already going through an ongoing process of adjusting to the demands made upon him/her in the search to preserve some sense of control and stability (i.e. he/she is adapting to the environment not so much so that he/she 'fits in' but that he/she survives). If the school demands changes in pupil behaviour which are inconsistent with the pupil's need for control and internal stability, then the pupil is not being helped.

- It may be useful to consider that pupils are conscripts to a system of education that has not been designed for them as individuals. Their behaviour and attainment are judged and reported by reference to age-related norms. Often they simply cannot succeed in this system. However, they can always make *progress* from their baseline. Do the school and parents value and recognise this progress often made in less than conducive circumstances?

The IE *Process* affords the opportunity for those concerned to try and understand school from the pupil's perspective so that for some of the time at least the pupil receives the individualised provision needed for progress to be made. Assessment for effective 'behavioural IEP planning' is a skilled activity for which whole-school and individual-staff development are essential. The following text and activities aim to support that development.

Assessment and identification: Principles

Summary

- Assessment procedures for IEP planning should be housed within the whole-school procedures for curriculum and assessment.

- Assessment for IEPs should be closely linked to purpose – that is, to record pupil progress, cause for concern, pupil strengths, targets and strategies.

- In order to reduce paperwork IEP assessment information should be reported in a focused evaluative style which briefly informs the next stage of planning.

How can IEPs be integrated into the school's general arrangements for assessing and recording the progress of all pupils?

(OFSTED 1996)

Problems experienced by schools in relation to assessment for IEPs suggest that schools see this as an *additional* time-consuming task. Schools do in fact have considerable information about pupils. Problems arise for staff involved in assessment for the Code of Practice if information on record about individual pupils is:

- only referred to when a pupil becomes a 'cause for concern' and is not used to inform forward planning;

- written in descriptive terms so that required information has to be extracted from an array of documentation;

- simply a written record which does not seek to address any specific questions such as 'what does this assessment information tell us about this pupil?' and ' how might we act on this information?'

Specific assessment requirements for the Code of Practice:

- Assessment information for the Code needs to be interpreted and analysed – particularly assessment which records response to specific interventions i.e. IEPs. Examining assessment information involves a process of problem solving which aims to inform the next stage of action – it is used for forward planning, not retrospective reporting.

- Summative assessment for the Code is prescribed to take place more frequently than the traditional yearly reports – normally reporting takes place termly to inform the next stage of action. Updating is thus a requirement which poses a particular challenge for those involved in IEPs as the original information cannot simply be erased and changed because it is needed for review meetings. IT can be a particularly useful tool to enable teachers to both save and edit existing IEP information, thus 'maintaining' the IEP as an active plan.

The challenge for schools is to ask themselves:

- What are our current assessment arrangements i.e. what information do we collect and at what intervals?

- How can we effectively extend or modify our existing assessment arrangements so that they support Code of Practice procedures?

For Stages 2 and 3 of the Code, the purpose of assessment can be seen to address the following questions:

	Question	Answer data	Action
Stage 1 Review Information	What progress has been made by the pupil at Stage 1 in relation to targets set?	Summary information from class teacher or year tutor. Minimum information could be 'good', 'satisfactory' or 'unsatisfactory'.	If unsatisfactory: seek additional advice and/or issue a Stage 2 IEP; otherwise continue at Stage 1 for two more review periods.
	How effective has the differentiation been at Stage 1?	Summary information from monitoring by class or subject teacher based on day-to-day response to Stage 1 provision. Child's and parents' views.	a) Continue? b) Modify targets? c) Modify strategies? d) Issue a Stage 2 IEP?
Stage 2 IEP Design	What 'different or extra' provision from that of Stage 1 does the child need?	Examples of pupil's response to tasks at Stage 1.	Review of provision at Stage 1 to check that there is a need for 'different or extra provision'.
	What are the new agreed areas of concern for this pupil?	Review of information gathered so far.	Agree targets.
	Under what conditions does the pupil learn/behave most effectively?	Pupil response to existing provision, including parental and child's views.	Identify and apply strategies.
Stage 2 IEP Review	What progress has been made by the pupil?	All summary information gathered so far.	Return to Stage 1 if concerns can now be addressed with Stage 1 provision or less. Otherwise continue at Stage 2 with or without new targets and strategies if satisfactory progress has been made. If not, design a Stage 3 IEP.
Stage 3 IEP Design	What additional provision or advice does the child or school need?	Examples of pupil's response to Stage 2 provision. Information and advice from identified outside agencies.	Review provision to ensure that outside agency involvement is needed. If not, implement a Stage 2 IEP.

	Question	Answer data	Action
	What are the agreed areas of concern for the pupil?	Review of existing information gathered so far plus advice from outside agencies or specialists.	Agree targets.
	Under what conditions does the pupil learn/behave most effectively?	Pupil response to existing provision plus the views of the parent, child and outside agency/specialist.	Identify and apply strategies in response to contribution from outside agencies.
Stage 3 IEP Review	What progress has been made by the pupil?	All summary information gathered so far.	Consider movement to Stage 2 if targets can be met with a Stage 2 IEP. If progress is satisfactory, continue with current stage. Otherwise adjust strategies and targets. If progress is still unsatisfactory, consult LEA to move to Stage 4.

For IEP planning, the *purpose* of assessment is to answer the following questions:

Question posed	Data needed to answer the question	Answer recorded on the IEP as:
What progress has the pupil objectives made towards achieving expected level (i.e. gap between 'observed' and 'expected' behaviour/attainment)?	Teacher assessment records across a range of subject areas. Check lists for expected/desired behaviours.	<ul><li>long- and medium-term</li><li>pupil strengths</li><li>draft targets and timescale for achievement</li><li>draft review dates.</li></ul>
What are the *agreed* areas of concern for this pupil?	Reports from parents, teachers, pupil perspective, outside agencies (if appropriate).	*agreed targets* (ensuring pupil and parent involvement and that targets set are relevant).
Under what conditions does the pupil exhibit the expected behaviour? If he is unable to exhibit the desired behaviour, the question becomes 'under which conditions is the frequency of the inappropriate behaviour reduced?'	This is addressed by comparing information collected from differing contexts, e.g. in class (structured, different subject areas, different teachers etc.) vs unstructured (playground setting) vs home, and by comparing differing perceptions of pupil behaviour.	<ul><li>strategies</li><li>*conditions* under which targets will be achieved.</li></ul>
What is the advantage for the pupil in keeping his/her present inappropriate behaviours/feelings?	Observation, pupil interview data, peer perceptions, teacher perceptions. Interpretation and analysis of the available assessment information to generate 'reasons' for pupil behaviour.	targets (carefully designed to meet pupil needs in a more acceptable way e.g. if pupil is exhibiting off-task behaviour in order to avoid failure, the target set must be designed accordingly).
What resources (human and physical) can be harnessed towards the achievement of targets?	Examination of in-school resources; home and community support, searching via Web sites, databases, support groups etc. Discuss with pupilthe 'who' and 'how' best to support.	<ul><li>*who* is involved in IEP i.e. roles and responsibilities – including those of pupil and parent</li><li>monitoring arrangements.</li></ul>

Assessment and identification: Institutional self-review

It follows that if procedures for the Code are going to be integrated into the school's existing procedures, the SMT need to ask:

- Do we collect the following information as part of our normal assessment procedures?
- If not, what additional information do we need to collect for EBD pupils?

Information	Action points
Records from previous schools	
Regularity of attendance	
National Curriculum attainments	
Standardised test results	
SATs	
Recorded achievements	
Reports on child in school settings	
Observations about the child's behaviour	
Parents' view of child's health and development	
Parents' perceptions of the child's response to school	
Parental information concerning factors which may be contributing to the child's difficulty	
Parental view concerning action that the school might take to help the child	
Child's perception of his/her difficulties	
Child's view of how he/she might best be helped in school	
Additional information from outside agencies e.g. Health, Social Services	
PUPIL'S RESPONSE TO STAGE 1 provision	
Information from medical practitioner	
Information from Social Services re: involvement with pupil	
Information from LEA re: education supervision order	
PUPIL RESPONSE TO STAGE 2 IEP	
Information from any other agency which is relevant to pupil in school	
PUPIL RESPONSE TO STAGE 3 IEP	

- Is assessment information written in descriptive reporting style or are attempts made to summarise information in such a way that it informs the next stage of planning?

- Is it clear to those concerned who is responsible for collecting, reporting and interpreting assessment of progress information needed for behavioural IEPs?

- Has the school examined other schools' procedures for collecting and collating assessment information for EBD pupils?

- Have the staff received training in assessment and recording for behavioural IEP planning?

- Is the school record keeping computerised? If so, could this be adapted to include additional information for IEP planning?

- Does the school have appropriate support materials for assessing EBD pupils (e.g. behavioural observation sheets, video, questionnaires for parents/pupils/peers, target and strategy banks, self-assessment sheets, commercially available checklists, national support group assessment guides etc.)?

- Do subject teachers include information about pupil learning, behaviour and individual characteristics in their reporting of pupil progress?

Assessment and identification: Ideas for action

Identify a pupil causing concern because of EBD. Locate available assessment information. Use that information to complete the table below. What are the barriers for teachers in 'assessing for behavioural IEP planning'? What are the implications for further development?

Work in pairs; discuss answer with colleague	Fill in the following:
What progress has the pupil made towards achieving expected level (i.e. gap between 'observed' and 'expected' behaviour/attainment)?	What are the: ● long- and medium-term objectives; ● pupil strengths; ● draft targets and timescale for achievement; ● draft review dates?
What are the *agreed* areas of concern for this pupil?	*agreed* targets (ensuring pupil and parent involvement and that targets set are relevant).
Under what conditions does the pupil exhibit the expected behaviour? If he is unable to exhibit the desired behaviour, the question becomes 'under which conditions is the frequency of the inappropriate behaviour reduced?'	● strategies ● *conditions* under which targets will be achieved.
What is the advantage for the pupil in keeping his/her present inappropriate behaviours/feelings?	targets (carefully designed to meet pupil needs in a more acceptable way e.g. if pupil is exhibiting off-task behaviour in order to avoid failure, the target set must be designed accordingly).
What resources (human and physical) can be harnessed towards the achievement of targets?	● *who* is involved in IEP i.e. roles and responsibilities – including those of pupil and parent ● monitoring arrangements.

Behavioural check sheet:

	Expected behaviour	Observed behaviour	Implication for IEP
Curriculum issues	Can work at same pace as peers.		
	Understands the language used in lessons.	(May respond better if curriculum is 'active', multisensory (particularly visual), structured etc. as in Science, ICT etc.)	
	Has literacy skills necessary to access and respond to curriculum.	(If not, further literacy assessment needed)	
	Has numeracy skills necessary to respond to the curriculum.	(If not, further assessment needed)	
	Has particular strengths which are used to achieve progress.		
The child as a learner	Has an intrinsic interest in topic/curriculum areas.	State which:	
	Is able to achieve some personally valued success without additional interventions.	State which:	
	Follows instructions given to the group.		
	Asks if doesn't understand.		
	Responds to teacher questions.		
	Sustains self-directed attention to task.		

Expected behaviour	Observed behaviour	Implication for IEP
Can retain information in short-term memory.		
Actively processes information (by taking notes etc.).		
Can self-monitor own behaviour.		
Perseveres to try and complete task.		
Can monitor own progress and 'knows when work is complete'.		
Brings appropriate equipment to lessons.		
Shows evidence of being able to self-'plan, do, review'.		
Is able to relate work given to his own interests and experiences (i.e. becomes involved).		
Extends learning activity beyond classroom by reading/self-study/homework.		
Can *generate* own responses (written and oral).		
Is able to work at the same speed as rest of class.		
Communicates with peers quietly in class.		

Relationships and social skills

Expected behaviour	Observed behaviour	Implication for IEP
Is able to ignore peer distractions.		
Will apologise when appropriate.		
Helps others when appropriate.		
Listens to others' conversation.		
Links his response to topic under discussion.		
Aware of the appropriate moment to contribute.		
Can 'read' facial expressions.		
Has an awareness of social conventions.		
Is able to turn take.		
Can interpret social communication language so that 'implicit' meaning is understood.		
Shows concern for others' feelings.		
Does not get pleasure from hearing others being told off or bullied.		
Can make eye contact when appropriate.		
Is aware that own behaviour has an effect on others – both good and bad.		

Emotional and affective behaviour

Expected behaviour	Observed behaviour	Implication for IEP
Can take responsibility for own behaviour.		
Can share possessions.		
Can share attention with group.		
Is sensitive, but not oversensitive, to criticism.		
Is able to give praise.		
Is able to receive praise.		
Uses failure to improve performance.		
Can handle peer pressure.		
Uses non-physical behaviour to express anger.		
Can decide upon a course of action.		
Knows and acknowledges own strengths and abilities.		
Is aware of weaknesses.		
Can sustain a course of action.		
Can take risks to achieve success (i.e. works to achieve success, not avoid failure).	(E.g. not 'can't do anything, no-one likes me' etc.)	

Expected behaviour	Observed behaviour	Implication for IEP
Uses 'relative', not 'absolute', reasoning.		
Can accept advice.		
Can work cooperatively.		
Can see things from another person's point of view.		
Can set realistic targets/aims.		
Is able to wait before acting.		
Is able to use self-control strategies.		
Is not a danger to self and seeks to avoid health hazards (smoking, drugs).		
Knows why he/she behaves the way he/she does.		
Is able to reflect and adjust accordingly. Knows which interventions have been helpful and why.		
Can apologise and mean it without prompting.		
Is able to ask for help, information.		
Is able to take blame.		
Can accept 'no' when appropriate.		

Expected behaviour	Observed behaviour	Implication for IEP
Can think positively.		
Can control negative thoughts.		
Has developed some appropriate strategies for coping with anxiety/stress.		
Actively enjoys some activities and relationships within the school setting.		
Can talk about feelings.	E.g. does not swear at teacher, spit in public etc.	
Acknowledges and responds to social conventions.		
Can tell the truth even if it may lead to punishment.		
Knows the difference between people not liking his/her behaviour and not liking him/her as a person.		
Can genuinely forgive others.		
Can trade short-term enjoyment for longer-term objectives.	(To what extent?)	
Can predict the consequences of own action and adjust behaviour accordingly.		
Can reward and recognise own success.		

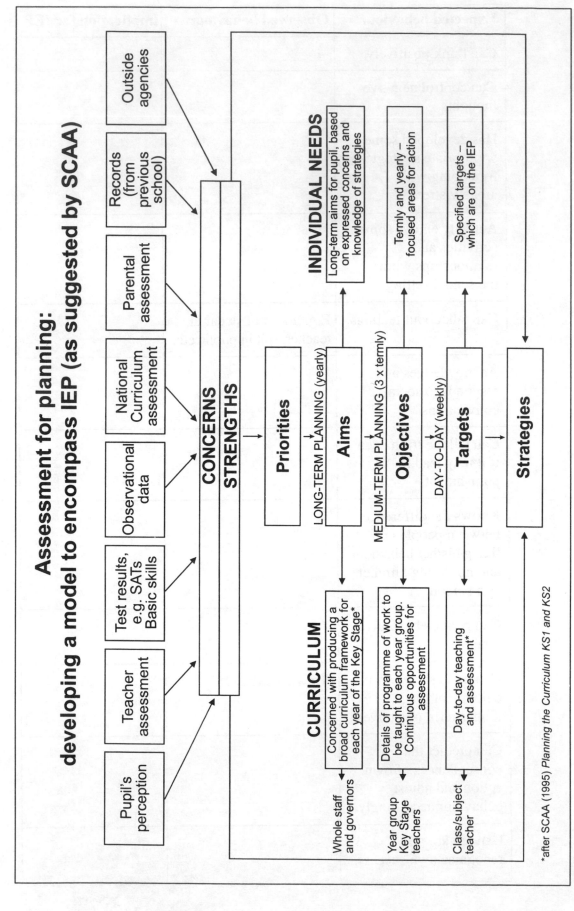

Assessment for planning:
developing a model to encompass IEP (as suggested by SCAA)

| Pupil's perception | Teacher assessment | Test results, e.g. SATs Basic skills | Observational data | National Curriculum assessment | Parental assessment | Records (from previous school) | Outside agencies |

CONCERNS
STRENGTHS

CURRICULUM

Priorities

LONG-TERM PLANNING (yearly)

Aims

Concerned with producing a broad curriculum framework for each year of the Key Stage*

Whole staff and governors

MEDIUM-TERM PLANNING (3 x termly)

Objectives

Details of programme of work to be taught to each year group. Continuous opportunities for assessment

Year group Key Stage teachers

DAY-TO-DAY (weekly)

Targets

Day-to-day teaching and assessment*

Class/subject teacher

Strategies

INDIVIDUAL NEEDS

Long-term aims for pupil, based on expressed concerns and knowledge of strategies

Termly and yearly – focused areas for action

Specified targets – which are on the IEP

*after SCAA (1995) *Planning the Curriculum KS1 and KS2*

Figure 4

36

Target setting and strategies: Principles

... central to the notion of IEP planning is the principle of setting learning outcomes in advance as targets to be attained within set time periods (written as what is to be learned, not how to increase the learning opportunities).

(SENJIT Schools Policy Pack 1995)

Purpose of targets

To:

- provide a focus for *coordinated educational effort* because everyone involved shares a common goal;
- strengthen the links between policy, planning and provision;
- provide a means for assessing the effectiveness of provision;
- support staff development in relation to SEN;
- provide realistic challenges;
- provide more rigorous criteria for the reporting of progress;
- establish agreed priorities of need.

Rationale

Target writing assumes that:

- what is learned can be broken down into its constituent parts;
- these parts can be described as distinct targets;
- these parts can be set out as a linear sequence;
- the final desired learning outcome can be achieved by meeting each sub-target in the sequence;
- methods of teaching can be identified from these targets.

Targets arise from the assessment of pupil progress within the curriculum and the individual profile of strengths and weaknesses. The *educational effectiveness* of targets rests on their design and selection as well as the shared belief of those involved that they are realistic and worthwhile. The setting of targets can provide a focus for the collaborative educational effort and may involve parents and learners. Furthermore, planning to achieve targets can direct attention to the efficient use of resources and the direct linking of teaching to learning outcomes.

The achievement of targets can be a measure of the effectiveness of IEPs and, therefore, of the school's SEN provision. It is important to remember, however, that targets do not exist independently. Setting them does not in itself achieve anything, neither does it necessarily result in effective teaching.

Possible pitfalls in writing targets

What has not yet emerged in the literature is the difficulty that most teachers have, whether specialist or not, in getting the children to make any progress with their IEPs after the teachers have written them. If the child does not make progress on their IEP there tends to be an assumption that there is something wrong with the child.

(McNamara and Moreton 1995)

- They can lead to a narrow focus for intervention (e.g. 'pupil to attend for five minutes') which does not link access and entitlement to the National Curriculum.

- They could lead to a false picture of 'effectiveness', i.e. many narrow 'behavioural' targets achieved over a short period of time may not be synonymous with real educational progress.

- They could lead to the assumption that *all* learning outcomes can be broken down into small steps. By focusing solely on these steps, one could lose sight of the overall outcome and might then believe that the steps themselves, when achieved, are the outcome.

- There is a danger that targets may be dictated by available resources rather than by pupil needs.

- They may be used manipulatively, e.g. if a school feels that a pupil needs additional resources, then targets could be selected to evidence 'slow' progress. Alternatively, 'progress' could be falsely speeded up by the selection of targets which are relatively easy for the pupil to achieve.

- The achievement of targets might become the *only* indicator of educational progress for the pupil and not be compared with progress made when he/she is not receiving 'different or extra' provision.

- Target setting might be facilitated in schools by selecting from a list 'relevant for EBD pupils'. While this may be part of a process of professional development for staff, it is important to be aware that this might lead to a 'label-deficit-cure model' pertinent to pre-Warnock thinking. Pupils with EBD may have been designated to a category but it cannot be assumed that they share needs. Targets must arise from an assessment of individual pupil progress and published schemes for target setting are a resource, not a solution.

Currently, there is an emphasis on SMART (*S*pecific, *M*anageable, *A*chievable, *R*elevant and *T*imed) (Lloyd and Berthelot 1992) targets with some LEAs prescribing that targets *must* fit these criteria. It should be stressed that this emphasis has sometimes fostered practice which is at odds with the principles of the Code of Practice in that it has lessened learning opportunities for the child, particularly if categorised as EBD.

Setting learning outcomes in advance as targets can be a sound principle for some aspects of teaching, particularly when the content of what has to be taught is highly structured. However, task analysis cannot and should not be used exclusively to generate IEP targets for EBD pupils. Targets for IEPs must be compatible with the meeting of medium- and long-term objectives.

The current favoured model is to provide teachers with guidance on how to write targets and then to provide them with lists of targets linked to categories of need. This method could be useful as a way of improving teacher competence in planning for SEN teaching, provided the aim is not simply to achieve 'technical competence' so that the IEP procedure can continue to be seen to be operational. The design and selection of educationally relevant targets require more than technical competence. They require at the very least a knowledge and understanding of individual differences in learning style and an understanding of the substantive issues surrounding teaching approaches which reduce curriculum complexity for the EBD pupil.

A 'key feature of effective school policies on special needs were: Practical Strategies for the identification and assessment of pupils, short, medium and long term difficulties, with clear expectations and advice for staff on writing IEPs.

(OFSTED 1996)

Types of targets

It might be useful to provide teachers with a taxonomy of 'targets'. These could fall under three categories as shown below:

- Direct linkage; learning outcome = target.

- Flexible linkage; target = range of possible learning outcomes.

- Indirect linkage; target = an outcome which can be recognised but not prescribed.

Alternatively, targets might be classified as:

- access targets;

- process targets;

- response targets;

- curriculum targets;

- personal development targets etc.

	Target = Direct linkage (learning outcome = target)	Target = Flexible linkage (range of possible learning outcomes)	Indirect linkage (outcome can be recognised but not prescribed)
Access	Will look at teacher when she uses his name.	Will make it known to the teacher if he does not understand.	Will self-direct his attention to the task given to him.
Process	Will listen to and repeat instructions given personally to him.	Will record information in a notebook when teacher is giving instructions.	Will join in class discussions.
Response	Will stay on task for period of time set on his book.	Will make a brief plan before starting to write and get this checked.	Will respond appropriately to teacher instructions.
Curriculum	Will mark six principal cities on a map of England.	Will make maps and plans of a real place.	Will enjoy reading.
Personal development targets (e.g. self-esteem)	Will use highlighter to direct his attention to work that he feels he has 'done well'.	Will use failure positively when guided by teacher.	Will direct thoughts and action more towards 'achieving success' rather than 'avoiding failure'.

In summary

Target setting for pupils experiencing EBD is a challenging task for teachers due to the fact that 'cause for concern' from which targets are generated is subject to the effects of environmental changes. A pupil may, for example, be responding to relatively unstable home events (e.g. the ups and downs of a discordant parental relationship) which, in turn, make his behaviour unpredictable. A target set one day may be irrelevant during the period of a week. Target achievement may also be unstable – due not to IEP inconsistencies but the effects of out of school factors. One key principle behind target setting as prescribed by the Code is the need to *measure* progress. Clearly, then, it is reasonable to deal with 'observable' outcomes, which is why EBD IEPs tend to be limited to such things as 'will increase attention to task'. However, for some EBD pupils (in particular, anxious pupils and those who *can* exhibit appropriate behaviour (i.e. they *can* direct attention to task) but have chosen *not* to in order to adapt to their difficulties), there is a need to address 'internal' non-observable cognitive activities such as their affective state, attributional style etc. In these cases, teachers may have identified a cause for concern but feel that they should target something else just because it can be written as an observable achievable target. Generating targets does become quicker with experience and teachers have made considerable progress in developing skills in SMART target writing. From this baseline, it is important that schools judge targets not just in terms of 'goodness of fit' with Code of Practice and LEA requirements for accountability but in terms of compatibility with the medium- and long-term aims for meeting the emotional and learning needs of the pupil concerned. For this reason, it is necessary for schools to look critically at their collective 'behavioural' IEP targets and the effect of style of target writing on pupil progress. While the accountability function of IEPs cannot be ignored, it should not take precedence over the educational function. For this reason, a 'balanced diet' of targets for EBD pupils (i.e. both affective and behavioural) is recommended.

Target setting and strategies: Institutional self-review

Target setting

Examine the targets contained within the school's behavioural IEPs.

Question	Implications for school development	Action
What is the ratio of behavioural to affective (emotional) targets?		
Are targets set compatible with medium- and long-term aims for the pupil concerned?		
Are targets concerned mainly with 'discipline and control'?		
Do targets translate into educationally relevant outcomes? Who is mainly responsible for EBD target setting (e.g. SENCO, pastoral care, class teacher, subject teacher)?		
Have pupils been involved in their own target setting?		
Are the targets set clear to all concerned?		
Are targets accompanied by criteria for how achievement of targets will be judged and by a clear statement of under what conditions?		
Does target progression reflect that pupils need to practise and generalise new behaviours in a range of settings?		
Do they address the 'different or extra' provision needed for pupils concerned?		
Do they avoid isolating and excluding the pupils concerned?		

Target setting and strategies: Ideas for action

Example of targets for Emotional and Behavioural Difficulties

Follow these guidelines in writing behaviour targets for the IEP:

STEP 1: Write down a behaviour which is opposite to and incompatible with the problem behaviour.
e.g. Problem behaviour = remains apart from other children.
Behavioural target = joins in activities with other children.

STEP 2: Use an active verb in the future tense to define the IEP target.
e.g. Behavioural target = sits at desk/table until asked to move by teacher.
IEP target = will sit at desk/table until asked to move by teacher.

STEP 3: Work on one behaviour at a time for a term, setting no more than three targets for each problem. Agree the targets with teacher, child and parent.
e.g. Description of problem = he is dependent on teacher.
Problem behaviours = i) constantly asks for readily available materials to be given to him before starting work; ii) constantly asks teacher for step by step instructions on how to begin/proceed with written work.
IEP targets = i) will take out all appropriate materials on request to start work; ii) when provided with clear instructions, will begin/proceed with written work independently.

STEP 4: Set IEP targets according to the hierarchy which you established in your problem profile.

STEP 5: Set targets for the central behaviour from the cluster of behaviours associated with it.
e.g. The cluster of problems = he hits other children, destroys other children's work, shouts out in lessons, refuses to start/complete work, swears at teacher, runs around the class.
The central behaviours = runs around the class and refuses to start/complete work (can be described as – out of control and failure to attend to tasks).
IEP targets = i) will sit quietly at the desk throughout lessons; ii) will walk around the classroom (only on request); iii) will start/complete work.

(SEN Resource Pack for Schools: McCarthy and Davies 1996)

Behavioural targets may not easily conform to a hierarchy unless *task analysis* is used to break the target down into smaller more achievable steps.

Target setting in the context of social interaction

The following tables show different mixes of activity and levels of social interaction which need to be considered when planning for teaching and playground activities:

	Alone Child may be colouring – adult initiated	*Parallel* Adult sits next to child and colours her own picture	*Group* Children are around a table all colouring/painting with adult(s)	*Interactive* Children are working together to produce a coloured picture/map for display with adult guidance
Adult				
Child/ pupil	Child is doing some maths in his workbook at a desk on his own	Children are sitting around a table doing their own maths work	A group of pupils are weighing sweets and putting them into marked packets	Pupils complete a survey about pocket money and how it is spent so that they can produce descriptive data about their class/ group spending habits

Dependent ————————————————————————————→ Independent

Structured	CA sits next to child and reads a book to him while he's playing in the sand	Child looks at book with adult	Child reads book to adult – told when to start and finish	Child reads silently in class when directed	Child selects a book from school library because he needs it for information to do homework	Child chooses a book and reads it for pleasure
Unstructured	Child plays with adult next to him	Child plays in playground with adult supervising	Child plays alone or watches TV unsupervised in house or classroom	Child plays next to other children with adult super-vision	Child plays in small group without direct adult supervision	Child plays cooperatively with other children without direct supervision

Ten key strategies (Blamires 1998)

Strategy 1:

Clarity of what is expected

Is the behaviour policy of the school made explicit through verbal and visual explanation? Does the learner know what the task is, how they have to do it, and when they have finished, what they have to do next? Docs the learner know the *implicit* routines of the school and class? Are areas with specific functions clearly marked? Does the learner know 'the way we do things here' and why? Does the child have a personal timetable so they know where they are in the day and during the week?

Strategy 2:

Predictability/Novelty

Is the day or lesson structured enough for the child or is it so structured it is monotonous and boring? Would different activities, groupings and stimuli increase the novelty of the activities?
Is enough happening to keep the child involved?

Strategy 3:

Affirmation/Criticism (reward system)

Are there opportunities to reward the real effort of an individual? Does the frequency of the reward need to be increased? Are the rewards given credible to the learner? Are opportunities for implied or overt negative criticism avoided (e.g. a request for child to perform their weakest skill in front of an unsympathetic audience of peers)? Are social rewards part of the system?

Strategy 4:

Interaction/Group work

Is flexible grouping in operation which avoids the negative effect of sink groups? Are learners able to work by themselves if required or seek the appropriate support from peers? Are learners encouraged to learn through group discussion and activity?

Strategy 5:

Available time for tasks (workload)

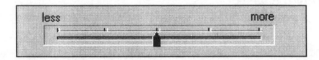

Is the workload appropriate for the learner? Has she too much or too little to do? Is the amount of time available for tasks, including homework, enough? Could the learner increase their work rate via the use of a laptop or computer?

Strategy 6:

Negotiation/Conflict (choice)

Does the learner have choice? Is she supported to develop independent learning and social skills? Are there opportunities for 'real' negotiation so that serious conflict can be avoided? Is there a flexible and fair system of negotiation available for all learners?

Strategy 7:

Level of work (complexity)

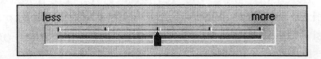

Is the work easy enough for the learner to do? Could it be broken down into smaller constituent tasks? On the other hand, does it set enough challenges? Are links made with other areas?

Strategy 8:

Modality

Are tasks set, undertaken and presented just using spoken language? Can multi-sensory approaches be applied? Can the preferred modality of the learner be emphasised?

Strategy 9:

Reading demand

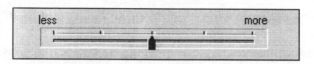

Is the reading demanded from the tasks appropriate? Is the readability level too difficult? Is the page layout of materials cluttered or too busy? Do key words need to be taught?

Strategy 10:

Attention (given or expected)

Does the child require extra monitoring and support by the teacher or support staff in order to keep on task? Can self-help skills and independence be developed?

Strategies and EBD IEP targets

The aim of this development activity is to consider strategies that may be used to meet frequently observed EBD IEP targets. Key points include:

- Targets should always be linked to long-term aims for a pupil's personal and educational development.

- Aims, targets, and strategies emerge out of a process of assessment of progress. They should not be 'taken off the shelf' but need to be adapted to meet the needs of the individual.

- 'New' behaviours need to be developed through the context of the pupil's everyday activity – i.e. *embedded* – at school that is through curriculum activity.

- As the pupil is emotionally wrapped up in his behaviour, it is useful to *depersonalise* the context in which targets are met. Often the whole-class setting can be used to develop more appropriate responses for one individual pupil.

- Any new learning experiences will need to be *structured and 'safe'* so that success is initially assured This may necessitate some withdrawal, small group, individual, specialist support intervention initially although strategies for generalising 'new' responses to classroom, playground settings have to be subsequently implemented as part of the IEP programme.

- Reasons for developing different or new responses must be made *explicit*.

- It is not sufficient to stop or prevent inappropriate behaviour – it needs to be replaced by behaviour which achieves a purpose relevant to the individual concerned *or* one which is antagonistic to it (e.g. anger cannot be experienced *simultaneously* with happiness).

- It is often not possible to replace inappropriate behaviour – it is thus realistic to target an increase in acceptable behaviour.

- Progress made should be charted from baseline (i.e. relative), not against norms for peers (i.e. absolute).

Aims	Targets	Strategies
To increase time spent cooperatively with peers.	To be able to take turns: • in a group • in a game • in a conversation.	LSA runs a group twice a week concentrating on our making *explicit* eye contact, using pupil names, pausing between turn taking etc. Get pupils to explain 'rules' to others. Try transferring to class activity (e.g. data collection for Maths project with pupils collecting information on, say, pocket money from peers and then working together to produce results for class presentation). For older pupils (PE lesson): watch football game to note contact and monitoring skills involved in collaborative activity towards an agreed end. Music: suggest pop music session to compose song/tune. Agree roles, need to adjust own performance for others etc. Video and assess the process, not the product. CDT: work on design together – discuss effectiveness of process and effect on final design – benefits of collaboration etc. Playground: once a week give small group a directed (but not adult monitored) activity e.g. 5-a-side, 5 minute netball, team object collections etc. Keep list of games so that children build up a bank of ideas to use when 'bored'.
To reduce aggressive outbursts.	To identify and report when anger/annoyance is triggered.	Depersonalise activity initially by using text (e.g. history, Shakespeare, stories to convey ideas. Class discuss and report when anger was triggered, built up etc. Practise saying (using the character as protection), 'I felt angry when . . . because . . .' Share what it feels like and what you would like to do to the person who caused the anger. Was the anger justified? Identify a time (playground or lesson), give pupils a 'cross/angry' token/sticker which they hand to the person concerned and walk off. At end of period, see who has given/received most stickers – discuss.

Aims	Targets	Strategies
	To develop one or two acceptable strategies for dealing with anger.	• Again, *depersonalise* activity by using an English lesson to write a booklet containing 'how to cope *safely* with anger'. Pupils' work is collated into one edition. This will give those pupils who haven't any strategies access to strategies used by non-EBD peers. • Use *safe, structured* activity in PSE by asking pupils to act out in pairs an incident. Ask 'audience' to identify which strategy they are using. • Develop *self-recognition* by selecting one week when all pupils keep a diary of when they did not cope well with anger. Count number of incidents. The next week, aim to reduce that number by at least one. • Extend activity by asking all pupils in class to say what triggered the incidents. Make this recognition *explicit*. • Ask pupils to identify times when they experience emotions which are *antagonistic* to feeling angry (e.g. happy, friendly, relaxed etc.). How can they increase these times by planning ahead? Arrange for pupils to use, apply and evaluate this strategy.
To reduce number of arguments with peers/teacher.	Increase use of negotiation strategies.	• *Depersonalise* by using class/group to problem solve e.g. how can we be fair when allocating computer time? (Use Maths lesson as context.) Use a History lesson to illustrate how an argument led to a war etc. • Identify some '*negotiation phrases*' which pupils have to begin their sentences: 'As we *both* can't have what we want, perhaps we could . . .' (State both sides.) 'As *you* want me to get on with my work which *I* can't do, would it be alright if I worked with Paul for the next ten minutes?' 'We could solve the problem by . . .' 'What if *I* . . . and *you* . . . ?' 'I am not going to let you have all your own way but I would agree to . . .' A bank of negotiation phrases is built up on index cards and when the teacher observes an argument, he/she offers the pupils concerned a choice from the cards. This replaces the 'stop arguing' command and gives the pupil a strategy to use.

Aims	Targets	Strategies
To improve development of attentional skills.	To recognise and respond to cued attention.	During class activity, teacher links to a cue card with instruction, 'I want you to listen to me and watch what I am doing.' (He/she holds up a sign with symbols 'teacher directs attention'.) 'Now if we look at your textbook, we will see . . .' (holds up symbol card for 'joint attention'). 'Now can you finish off your work?' (holds up cue card for 'self-directed attention'). The aim is to get pupils to recognise that there are different types of attention and that they can be cued into the appropriate attentional style. Instead of the teacher constantly nagging the pupil, she can use the pupil's name plus a cue card to signal and reward appropriate attention.
To increase participation in class activities.	To ask relevant questions in class.	Asking questions is difficult for some pupils because questions have to be *generated at speed*, are *personal* and *public* and *carry the risk* that others will find out that the pupil doesn't understand. This skill can be acquired in a controlled, depersonalised way initially by the teacher giving out a set of questions on cards such as, 'Can you explain again what we have to do?', 'How much do we have to write?' or questions specific to the subject such as, 'Why did we have to boil the liquid first?' (Teachers familiar with their subject area will know the typical questions or areas of difficulty.) At points throughout the lesson the teacher can ask, 'Any questions?' and those pupils with cards can read out their question, get an answer and then be rewarded: 'Thank you for asking that question. Once pupils can cope with asking depersonalised questions and realise that failure or ridicule is not inevitable, this strategy can be developed further until the targeted pupil is able to contribute in class.

Aims	Targets	Strategies
To reduce fear of failure.	To use failure to improve performance.	Clearly, it is not failure which adversely affects pupil progress but the pupil's reaction to it. It is necessary to *depersonalise* it by saying, 'Some of you' (even if it is only one pupil) 'made the mistake of . . . It is useful that you did this because it means that I need to go over it and explain it more clearly'. The aim is to make *explicit* to the pupil that mistakes can lead to greater understanding and improved performance if they are *used positively*. Marking is an important medium for giving information and feedback in response to errors e.g. instead of marking spelling errors in red, the teacher could say, 'Could you find three spelling mistakes and correct them?' The pupil will then be rewarded for response to initial failure. Circle time or assessment activity allows an opportunity for peers to 'look at the work of the person next to you and say two good things about it and one way in which it could be made better'. The pupil then hears his own peers give 'balanced' responses to his work, plus there is guidance on how to improve. Pupils can be asked to watch a football match over the weekend, identify a player and write three good things about his performance and how he could use mistakes made to make his game better next time.

Coordination and monitoring: Principles

Summary

- Coordination and monitoring is not the sole remit of the SENCO but involves the allocation of roles and responsibilities for all concerned.

- Coordination and monitoring of IEPs must be integrated into whole-school procedures.

- The SENCO has a key role in monitoring the effectiveness of the systems and procedures by tracking the impact on pupils' progress.

- The efficiency of the coordination and monitoring systems depends upon the level of commitment of the school management to meeting diverse needs.

- The effectiveness of the SENCO depends upon the status allocated, resources and the support given.

- Effective coordination of IEPs cannot occur unless supported by efficient and focused school management strategies.

- Coordination and monitoring of IEPs should not be divorced from pastoral care and the school's behaviour policy.

- Strategies for monitoring and coordination should be compatible with the school's SEN policy and should 'have regard to' the principles inherent in the Code of Practice.

- The fragile and transient nature of EBD is such that a greater degree of skill and flexibility is required to take account of the effect of events outside of the school on pupil learning and behaviour. Procedures prescribed by the Code of Practice may need adjustment if the needs of pupils experiencing EBD are to be met.

The successful implementation of that plan is brought about by the skill of the coordinator, support from school management, flexibility and commitment from all. Monitoring pupils' progress, particularly the medium-term progress, through this plan requires equal levels of commitment, collaboration and thought to make it effective. Pupils' general behaviour, attitudes and personal development and the Spiritual, Moral, Social and Cultural curriculum play an important role in the development of effective IEPs for pupils experiencing EBD. These are the responsibility of *all members of staff* with support from the SENCO. To achieve this, we are going to consider:

- the importance of monitoring and evaluating practice in order to promote a coherent cycle of planning in the *short, medium and long terms* (Institutional self-review – see later in this section);

- a review of the professional skills required to
  (a) work successfully together to maintain consistency and focus the educational effort involved
  (b) support and enable others to do so from an organisational point of view;

- information derived from analysing the learning environment through monitoring and the choices that a SENCO will face with colleagues;

- ways in which monitoring and coordination of IEPs will have consequences for whole-school development;

- the *level of interpersonal and management skills of staff* (including head teacher and SENCO) and how this will have an impact on efficient coordination of the educational effort for IEPs, and that this influence too should be monitored.

Ideally, the SENCO should be a member of the school management team and have time allocated away from classroom teaching in order to facilitate important whole-school innovations and responses, particularly for pupils experiencing EBD. In this part of the book, the role and skills of a SENCO are considered alongside the relationship between colleagues working together to bring IEPs to fruition for the benefit of pupils. The Code of Practice (Department for Education 1994) clearly states seven major areas that the SENCO is responsible for in the school. It is a central pivot for monitoring consistency and cohesion in the school's approach to pupils experiencing EBD, through the IEPs. It is a responsible and occasionally insecure role within a school, depending on the relationship between the SENCO, the staff and the school management team. Senior management has a vital role in providing high quality leadership within schools, and in managing effectively a range of tasks (including timetabling, providing support for staff, liaising with parents, governors, the LEA etc.) that influence behaviour within schools. This does not mean, for example, that a school can eliminate social disadvantage, but a disadvantaged child attending a school with effective IEP arrangements may do better than a more advantaged child attending a school with ineffective arrangements. Schools can influence the behaviour, the standard of work and the life chances of a child. To a significant degree, the success of the SENCO depends upon some fundamental conditions being in place.

Again, there are particular problems for the SENCO or other key members of staff in that pupils experiencing EBD rarely proceed through these steps at a measured or measurable pace. The factors at work outside a child often have far greater importance in shaping their behaviour than those inside the child and the nature of support is sometimes difficult to pin down. For example:

Bereavement	Ethnic differences and discrimination
Adoption or fostering	Homelessness
Others' attitudes towards disabled parents	Living with mentally ill parent(s)
Divorce or separation	Rejection by peers
Bullying (by adults or children)	Harassment
Violence at home	Addiction in the home
Lack of school ethos or rules	Lack of appropriate or satisfactory
Teachers' lack of training and status	facilities or resources
Unrealistic expectations	Lack of pastoral (or child) care

Difficult decisions have to be made about the nature of the support required in school and often referral for outside help, say, from a counsellor or school psychological services, develops more rapidly than the ability of services to respond (even if those services are available to the child or school). Although the school is asked to clearly state when assessment is needed and make arrangements in an orderly fashion, the needs of the moment often put great pressure on all concerned. It is vitally important in this situation that a school has a robust and consensual approach with effective policies and guidelines, combined with good relationships and a well thought out ethos concerning relationships, behaviour, attitudes and personal development of its pupils. This, in turn, makes the notion of 'early intervention and assessment' even more crucial and one that requires considerable skill and knowledge of the pupil in order to be aware of, or forecast, potential difficulties.

In order not to be continually reactive in this area, the school management or the SENCO or key worker should attempt to establish useful links with outside agencies as an ongoing process. The next step is to seek outside advice and this then sets in motion a process of referral. Mainstream schools need a framework which would incorporate a clear policy, early identification of EBD, interventions with stated aims, and a simple and clear set of procedures that are known to all.

The referral process

Step 1: Referral and the first question is, 'Who do you refer to?'

The first step in supporting schools is usually reducing anxiety among staff, by letting them know that somebody else knows about their difficulties. In addition to establishing as many ongoing links as possible, the school needs to actively solicit information relevant to children with EBD, from agencies such as counselling services, family support groups or centres, and also other relevant bodies, such as local groups dealing with alcoholism or drug abuse, parents' or special needs action (support) groups, support groups for fostered children, or groups growing out of the need for knowledge about medical syndromes such as Attention Deficit Disorder (ADD).

Step 2: Consultation and observation

Consultation is a time for the support service, consultant or outside agency to listen, when schools and their staff express their concerns. It may be necessary for outside personnel to meet the appropriate school staff, collect information, make some observations and arrange a meeting within a set time to plan for the future. The school staff and SENCO should think about the pupil's broad emotional and behavioural needs and possible short-term targets. Parents, social workers and any other appropriate agencies should be invited to the joint planning meeting. Issues around the pupil's attendance or the pupil's views will also be discussed here.

Step 3: Joint planning

The joint planning meeting should underpin all subsequent work. Exactly how it goes will depend on whether the school assessment is at Stage 2 or 3. This meeting should be well prepared and this depends a great deal on the effectiveness of the existing IEP planning and evaluation. If it is good, people will know what to expect and the meeting will be more effective. Time boundaries are as important as clear outcomes. The pupil's broad emotional and behavioural needs can be outlined and realistic, short-term, meaningful targets identified.

The real work, however, is done in negotiating the process; the 'who does what, where, when and how' and it is important to reflect this in the IEP somewhere so that proper evaluation of the response to the problem is recorded. Often the recording does not monitor the *effectiveness* of any outside interventions, only that it has happened. This is part of the unwanted game of 'giving away' the problems into someone else's lap. It is essential that parents and other agencies are included in the planning (e.g. SSA, EWO, RSW, EP, Soc. W, SENCO) and that all relevant parties, including the class teacher, *remain* responsible for their part in the process. This will be determined by:

- the pupil's educational needs;

- the teacher's need to make the curriculum available;

- the educational target(s) and outcomes decided upon;

- available resources.

The teacher will alter the teaching, differentiate the work and the organisational aspects of the classroom, as appropriate. Immediate support could be in-class, whole class, small group, social skills work, individual, staff supervision, INSET or part-time placement at a pupil referral unit. Support from other agencies might involve the Education Welfare Officer, speech therapy, counselling, child guidance, medical and specialist medical advice, to name but a few. The sources of support will vary from area to area of the country and according to the needs of the pupil but it is vital that the effectiveness of the support in reaching the agreed targets and in supporting the child's educational development is clearly evaluated. Once the process is agreed and everyone is aware of their role, it is formally recorded and logged on the IEP. This process is integrally linked to the writing of IEPs and to daily planning. The major success of joint planning is that it gives staff time to *think* and provides an opportunity to develop a *response* to behaviour rather than a *reaction* to it.

Step 4: Monitoring and review

The joint planning meetings should always set a review date which is also logged and evaluated on the IEP. Particularly for a school, pupil or parent new to the process, regular reviews are important (for example, to be set within two weeks of the joint plan). This helps support and encourage. It irons out any minor difficulties and keeps communication open. The termly or half-termly review process is much easier to conduct and assess as it is directly related to the targets set. So, too, the process is reviewed. It becomes clear who has done what, how, where and when and what the results are. The teacher's daily planning and assessment of progress is crucial to the refining of IEP targets at all stages in this process. Given that a statement has 'annual targets', the whole cycle should fit together as one continuous process (see section on assessment and identification).

Coordination and monitoring: Institutional self-review

Monitoring and evaluation can have two overall focuses:

- approaches that attempt to analyse the learner;
- approaches that analyse learning tasks and the learning environment.

Analysing the learning environment

This is one of the most important tasks for the key members of staff who are responsible for coordinating the relevant IEPs. Usually it is the SENCO who will coordinate the IEPs but should not be responsible for completing all of them. The reason for this becomes more obvious when the reasons for achieving a balanced assessment and hence a balanced IEP come from approaches that analyse the learning environment and tasks as well as the pupil.

A carefully constructed IEP can emphasise natural means of gathering information by informal observation, questioning and discussion. These are the strategies that effective teachers have used since schools were invented. It is vital that assessment is ongoing, linked to daily planning and integral to the evaluation of lessons and differentiation strategies, however simple or complex these arrangements might be. The IEP is one way to integrate assessment of progress and the recording of developments or changes into the curriculum. If they are to be part of a plan which attempts to make teaching and learning more effective, then there must be a proper element of evaluation in the actual form but, more importantly, in the comments that teachers make completing the forms.

Organisational change

Implementing organisational change, even with clear goals and plans of action, is a very complex process. In order to grow and develop, particularly in terms of expecting staff to develop their abilities and commitment to recording progress for individual pupils through IEPs, there will need to be some organisational or group changes in attitudes, skills and understanding.

Sometimes the SENCO or other responsible person will find it necessary to motivate change in order to set up a satisfactory system for coordinating and monitoring IEPs. To *energise changes*, it might be necessary to:

- identify surface dissatisfaction with present system;
- ensure overall participation in change;
- reward behaviour in support of change;
- make time and opportunity to prepare and disengage from present way(s) of doing

things or seeing things (people get stuck in their ways and they often need a little time to consider what is happening).

Teamwork

The relationship between the functioning of an effective team and its effect on both pupils and adults in schools and units is a mutual one. Positive social behaviour, to gain access to learning for young people, is influenced by the 'models' provided by adults which in turn dictate the 'school culture' and ethos. However, our focus is on IEPs and, when teamwork is good, group life is enriched by positive and enthusiastic interchange on a regular basis and there are many opportunities to share and develop the valuable information that IEPs can give. It is also more efficient to share and develop consistent practices across a school – it radically reduces the individual effort in the long run. It is important to see how teamwork will support the preparation, development and implementation of effective IEPs; some of the main characteristics, requirements and advantages of good teamwork include:

- the *creation of a 'sense of purpose'* and motivation of others through focusing your own goals and action plans. Use these skills to help others' focus on targets for pupils;

- the *giving and taking of criticism* with a positive and supportive attitude and encouraging others to do likewise. Discussion and moderation of targets and evaluation of progress will benefit from this;

- the development of good *active listening skills*, encouraging others' contributions and making them feel worthwhile;

- the willingness to *give positive feedback* to other people's ideas;

- the clear understanding of *your own role* in the school or unit and the team;

- the *development of motivation and confidence* through contributing to discussion around pupils' progress and their IEPs;

- the willingness to *disagree with clear reasons*, not to 'block' but 'move on'. This is important when dealing with other outside agencies where commitment is difficult to obtain;

- the *review of your own self-management* (time, stress, assertiveness, communication), just in case you are blaming others for your own deficiencies;

- the assessment of your own *training/skill and personal development* needs for effectiveness;

- the willingness to modify your personal agenda and negotiate in meetings;

- the generation of clear learning, group, team (or departmental) goals and/or objectives. This will help both the writing of IEPs for pupils and your ability to move things to support that IEP;

- *agreement on how to manage disruption*, 'opting out' or conflict with adults as well as pupils;

- the encouragement of problem solving and creativity within the team, and *accepting other views*;

- creating realistic and achievable action plans for future work/development;

- taking time to plan the effective use of existing resources and time;

- the use of goal planning and consensus to identify need for resources for pupils and INSET for yourself.

No list such as this is complete. There will inevitably be many barriers to communication on both an interpersonal and whole-school front that will make IEPs more time-consuming and their monitoring more difficult.

Coordination and monitoring: Ideas for action

Who does what with whom?

SENCO works *with colleagues* to *monitor* the effect *of* the IEP and the effect *on* the IEP for EBD

SENCO and/or 'key' personnel for pastoral care, EBD and behaviour	Classroom or Learning Support assistants Monitor . . .	Head and senior management (inc. governors) Monitor . . .	Outside agencies and professions Monitor. . .	Teaching colleagues Monitor. . .
The day-to-day operation of the school's SEN, pastoral and behaviour policies	The general arrangements in school for playtimes or breaktimes and their influences on behaviour.	Focus on efficient use of IEP in meetings, conferences or in collaboration between staff in achieving policy aims and intentions.	The arrangements for outside interventions and the way these are recorded and integrated onto the IEP.	The impact of class teaching on pupil's progress and attainment in specific subjects or activities. Pupil's responses to teaching and recording these.
Liaising with and advising fellow teachers	Deployment of CAs/LSAs and the requirements for daily information to be collated for IEPs.	Sensitive arrangements for consistent recording of difficult incidents or general progress towards IEP targets.	Working out special arrangements (e.g. timetable) with teachers for outside interventions or professional visits.	Access strategies, differentiation of lessons and activities – pupil responses recorded on IEP and evaluated.
Coordinating provision for children experiencing EBD	What is the CAs/LSAs role? In classroom? In the school during playtimes/lunch?	Sufficient allocation and efficient management of resources to support IEP targets for EBD.	Ensuring confidentiality and good professional collaboration. Protecting educational priorities on IEP.	The implementation of IEP targets in lessons through effective teaching practices. Efficient day-to-day assessment towards IEP targets.
Maintaining the school's SEN register and overseeing the records on all pupils with EBD	The 'flow' of information from the IEP(s) to individual CAs/LSAs to support focused and additional teaching activity.	Good information coming from IEPs to support legal requirements for annual review. Matching IEP targets with efficient use of resources.	Regular reviews of concerns or progress stemming from outside interventions. The impact of other interventions on progress towards IEP targets.	The arrangements for teachers to show concerns stemming from IEP-related activities. The flow of information about IEPs and special arrangements.

SENCO and/or 'key' personnel for pastoral care, EBD and behaviour	Classroom or Learning Support assistants Monitor . . .	Head and senior management (inc. governors) Monitor . . .	Outside agencies and professions Monitor. . .	Teaching colleagues Monitor. . .
Liaising with the parents of children with EBD	Direct lines of communication with parents – nature of guidance. Daily links with parents through Home Books etc. – links with IEP arrangements and targets.	The flow of information from the school in general to parents. Involvement of SMT with appropriate and prearranged activities or interventions to support IEP targets.	IEP targets and information and match with information to parents about specialist groups or support.	Accuracy and sensitivity of reporting to parents and progress towards IEP targets. Relaying of parental concerns quickly and sensitively. Positive responses to parent concerns.
Contributing to in-service training of all staff in matters relating to EBD	Training needs in relation to IEP targets and common elements. Arrange INSET.	The sufficiency and targeting of resources for training on IEP-related areas. Advise SMT/GB on this.	The group or common IEP elements or targets – match outside trainers or consultants to staff needs in these areas.	Training needs in relation to IEP targets and common elements. Arrange INSET.

Monitoring and coordinating IEPs

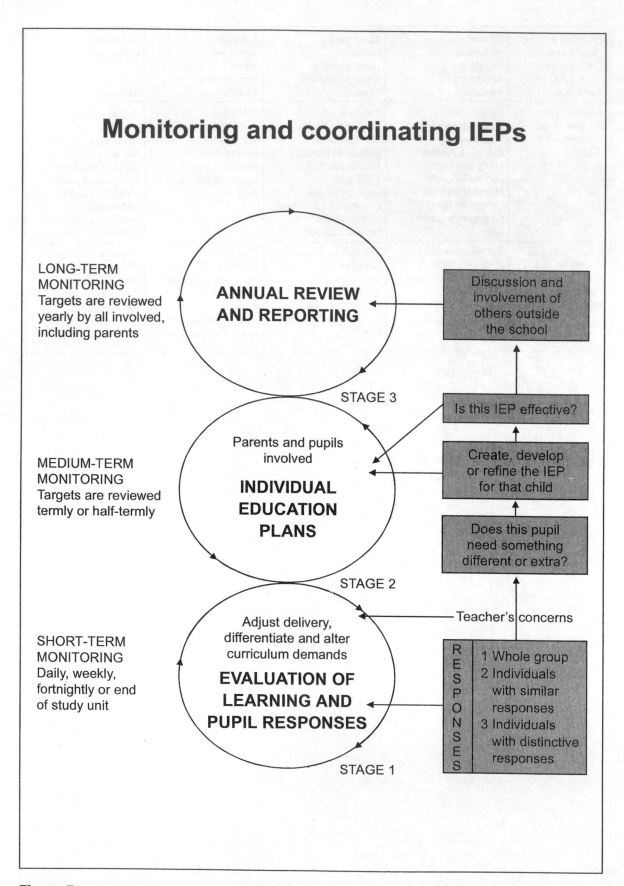

LONG-TERM
MONITORING
Targets are reviewed
yearly by all involved,
including parents

**ANNUAL REVIEW
AND REPORTING**

Discussion and
involvement of
others outside
the school

STAGE 3

Is this IEP effective?

MEDIUM-TERM
MONITORING
Targets are reviewed
termly or half-termly

Parents and pupils
involved

**INDIVIDUAL
EDUCATION
PLANS**

Create, develop
or refine the IEP
for that child

Does this pupil
need something
different or extra?

STAGE 2

Teacher's concerns

SHORT-TERM
MONITORING
Daily, weekly,
fortnightly or end
of study unit

Adjust delivery,
differentiate and alter
curriculum demands

**EVALUATION OF
LEARNING AND
PUPIL RESPONSES**

R E S P O N S E S

1 Whole group
2 Individuals
   with similar
   responses
3 Individuals
   with distinctive
   responses

STAGE 1

Figure 5

62

Monitoring the impact of school management on IEPs

Monitor IEP support	Monitor activities	Review effectiveness (1) Established well (2) Need development (3) Comments . . .
Overall school management	● establishing and maintaining internal and external communication systems	
	● staff management	
	● fostering a sense of community	
	● taking the lead in setting aims and standards	
	● supporting staff	
	● directing overall curriculum and organisational planning	
	● establishing the reasons for rules	
	● encouraging collective responsibility	
	● outlining the affective curriculum	
	● providing models of behaviour	
	● consistent with the RE and PSHE policies of the school	
Successful behaviour policies	● based on a clear and defensible set of principles or values	
	● have a minimum number of enforceable rules	
	● specific to each school	
	● strike a healthy balance between reward and punishment	
	● reserve the most severe punishments e.g. exclusion, for the most serious offences e.g. violence	
	● allow for flexibility in the administration of punishments to take account of individual needs	
Consistency with IEP targets . . .	● avoid the punishment of whole groups	
	● avoid punishments which humiliate pupils	
	● recognise the importance of the role of parents and of ancillary staff	
	● apply to school activities on and off site	
Particular incidents affecting IEP targets	● be alert to signs of bullying and racial harassment	

	• deal firmly but consistently with provocativebehaviour	
Pastoral care and personal development	• senior pastoral staff should spend more time advising and supporting other colleagues, and minor behaviour problems should be dealt with by class or form teachers	
	• tutor periods should be used well, rather than just being seen as a time-killing exercise	
	• the pastoral system should also be used to provide feedback on pupils' views	
	• good communication links should be developed between pastoral staff and support services	
	• continuing professional development should develop teachers' basic counselling and interpersonal skills	
	• senior pastoral staff should have more in-depth training or qualifications in this area	

Coordinating through the IEP

Look at the example of an IEP on the next page. Be critical of the layout and content. What do you think of its usefulness? How does the design of this IEP reflect, for example, the following?

- recording parents' or pupils' views and contributions;

- evaluating the responses of outside professionals and their effectiveness;

- enabling the school to match the support given to academic success and progress;

- the use of information to monitor the differentiation of lessons or learning activities;

- information to monitor the medium-term progress of pupils;

- information to refine longer-term educational targets;

- triggers and/or steps in the referral process;

- the extent of outside agency involvement;

- the quality and focus of outside professionals' interventions.

Code of Practice: Individual Education Plan

Individual Educational Plan for:		DOB:	NC Year:	Level Statement

Term 19	Key members of staff

Nature of the child's learning difficulty:

Provision made:	Staff involved:

Involvement of other agencies/external specialists including frequency and timing of support:

Specific curricular programmes (including NC requirements) and learning activities and strategies to be used:

Materials:	Equipment:

Targets to be achieved:

By:

Help from parents at home:	Pastoral care or medical requirements:

Monitoring and assessment arrangements:	Review date:
	Signed...Head Teacher
	....Special Educational Needs Coordinator

Involving the learner: Principles

Children with emotional and behavioural difficulties cover the range of ability found in mainstream schools but generally behave unusually or in an extreme fashion to a variety of social, personal, emotional or physical circumstances.

(Department for Education 1994)

Summary

- Children with EBD cover the range of ability found in mainstream schools.

- It is necessary to understand some of the underlying reasons for EBD in order to set appropriate targets and monitor progress.

- The whole of the curriculum and organisation of the school must contribute towards the growth of personal responsibilities and good personal relationships.

- The behavioural approach should be seen as a short-term strategy to get access to the learning environment. A rigid adherence to only behavioural approaches is unlikely to promote longer-term personal and social development.

- There is a risk that personal predispositions can influence the way in which the IEP is constructed; it is therefore advisable to institute regular joint reviews.

- Acting on attitudes, beliefs, capabilities and feelings will have a greater impact in the long run than directing attention to specific inappropriate behaviours.

- If targets are not embedded within the context of a curriculum, then medium- and longer-term progress will not be monitored.

- The pupil is a person who needs to experience some personal success – not an educational statistic whose function in the school is to contribute to the school's PICSI (Pre-Inspection Context and School Indicator) profile.

- There is a danger that teachers can damage the feeling of competence and confidence by judging pupils purely on the basis of their behaviour and background.

- The individual pupil can *learn* how to change if taught appropriately.

- A distinction needs to be made between the management of a pupil (teacher target) and the setting of relevant learning objectives (pupil targets).

In this section, the primary concern is to gain some understanding of the internal factors and circumstances at work within the learner and to do three things with this knowledge:

- to understand and be able to use appropriate language and descriptors of learners' needs to generate both targets *and evaluative statements* for IEPs;

- to match the learners' needs with appropriate planned action by the teacher and the school, through the IEPs;

- to make certain that the learners' progress is charted in a meaningful way in the context of longer-term curriculum goals and to raise their standard of academic success.

. . . the whole of the curriculum and organisation of the school must contribute towards the growth of personal responsibilities and good personal relationships . . .

(Warnock 1977)

Becoming competent

This is a complex process, involving many factors within the learner and many in the situation that the learner finds him or herself. When we add to that the interaction between teacher and learner, the whole thing becomes even more complex, dynamic and subject to many, many influences. A lot of the time we have to work intuitively and often we work on *implicit assumptions* about what is happening with us and with the learner. This is good, up to a point, but as any athlete will tell you, in order to improve our competence, skills and understanding, it is necessary to become aware of areas for further development in ourselves. It is also vital that we recognise and make clear our existing skills and abilities. We can then develop confidence from this knowledge *and celebrate our own competence*. This is very important, especially in this very demanding area of work.

The school environment demands from all those who function within it a set of acceptable behaviours which are learned through a process of socialisation and are specific to the culture and situation of the school. The process of socialisation is a complex and subtle one, through which a child develops from a demanding and dependent baby into a productive and integrated member of society. This process involves personal, social, emotional, moral, spiritual and cultural development and growth throughout the time at school. It does not come from strictly behavioural interventions, although these may be useful in the short term. A pupil has to extract from rules and guidance how to behave but needs to *learn* more long-term strategies and beliefs in order to become a mature member of his or her community. Guidance, frameworks, resources, curriculum-based schemes of work and learning targets that support learning and growth in these aspects of a pupil's learning are on the increase. Some examples of these are shown opposite.

In thinking about the complex process of becoming socially skilled, it is worth considering the following points:

- that the skills are acquired either before pupils enter full-time education or during it;

- that the learning of these skills depends upon opportunity, motivation, role modelling and a secure environment to practise in;

- successes and rewards will make experiences that are likely to be different for children from different backgrounds, cultures and family composition.

- some of these social skills are manifested in more suitable ways such as body posture and eye contact; they may be related to cultural expectations with which we are unfamiliar;

- individual pupils may not be armed with sufficient control or skills to be able to resist pressures or attacks to their own integrity, leading to outbursts which may be a 'one-off' but serious.

Guidance, learning resources and schemes of work – some examples (see Bibliography for details)

Personal, social and emotional	Moral (inc. behaviour)	Spiritual (inc. RE)	Cultural	Health
QCA SMSC Curriculum	QCA SMSC Curriculum	QCA SMSC Curriculum	QCA SMSC Curriculum	Health Promoting Schools Award (HPSA)
Instrumental Enrichment Programmes (Feuerstein 1969)	Instrumental Enrichment Programmes (Feuerstein 1977)			*Liking Myself* (Palmer 1997)
OFSTED Framework	OFSTED Framework	OFSTED Framework	OFSTED Framework	*100 Ways to Enhance Self-Esteem in the Classroom* (Canfield and Wells 1976)
The Peer Tutoring Handbook: Promoting Co-operative Learning (Topping 1988)	Developmental Group Work (Thacker 1984)			*Liking Myself* (Palmer 1977)
Learning Through Talk – INSET on Oracy			Learning Through Talk – INSET on Oracy	*Self-Esteem: A Classroom Affair* (Borba and Borba 1978)
Circle Time (Curry & Bromfield)				*Drama Therapy: Theory and Practice* (Jennings 1992)
Games for Social Skills (Bond)				
The High/Scope Training Programme	The High/Scope Training Programme			

The process of becoming competent in social skills

When we attempt to become more competent, whether it is in 'adding up' or classroom management skills, there is always a risk involved and surprises. Applying the model to the acquisition of social skills illustrates the fact that a pupil may, at the start, be totally unaware of his incompetence, for example, in handling criticism from others. He may snap back when comments are made. There are skills involved in handling criticism (e.g. taking out some bits but accepting others) and the first step is to raise awareness of this possibility with the pupil and derive targets for learning the skills.

'Behaviour' targets for IEPs

Most of the practical support literature for teachers seems to revolve around a behavioural approach with its characteristic language of rewards, sanctions, contingent praise, observable behaviours, timed and frequency observations of behaviour. So, it is not surprising that short-term targets and even medium-term (IEP) targets are often phrased in the language of the behavioural approach.

IEPs are not meant to be short-term (although they are refined by short-term assessment of progress) and they need to be able to reflect progress, not only in curriculum or learning terms, but to be *embedded in a continuum of progress*. The problem with 'behavioural targets' is that they are short-term and leave teachers with the problem of 'what next?' Does the programme just grind to a halt or do we cut it off when the pupil has satisfied us that he has achieved these short-term goals for a 'reward'? Or do we have to invent a whole curriculum for each pupil who is disaffected or disruptive or challenging?

This approach has been used because it is quick and shows some immediate (but rarely embedded) results. No matter which way you slice it, a *strict and limited behavioural approach* is more fitted to dog training than to an educational environment, being based upon reaction and dependence (being a reactive learner). The more educational concepts of action, anticipation, reason, example, discussion, discovery, and independent learning (that fully involves the learner) are more appropriate in the classroom. Behaviour will then be led by the skills, beliefs and the educational environment itself. *The behavioural approach should be seen as short-term strategies to get access to the learning environment.* When this is achieved, there is still more work to be done in providing equal opportunities to learn in the personal, social, spiritual, moral and cultural domain (just as with the subject-based curriculum).

In the list below, there is only one aspect of 'behavioural approaches' that does not involve the person's internal construction of the world around him or her or the effect of behaviour on the environment. We are not reactive beings, we are curious, adaptive and anticipatory in our make-up. Behaviour has become a much used term in education and covers a multitude of assumptions and value judgements. The word behaviour is nearly always preceded by a qualifying description (strange, characteristic) or a value judgement (bad, good) or by a qualifying adjective (funny, sad).

Behaviour and access to learning

Behaviour

- *is what is observable*
- is active
- affects others
- causes reactions
- alters the situation
- changes the circumstances
- is based on predictions
- is shaped by anticipation
- is driven by internal and external events

Behavioural targets represent nothing more than *initial strategies to give access to learning* for pupils who find it hard to conform or to function in a group or to take part in the lessons and educational activities that a school provides. The behavioural approach may be suitable for immediate classroom management in a limited way, but not for the longer-term growth and development of children. IEPs and their targets for the learner should be established within a longer-term framework that enables children to develop from early years to teenage years.

The way we think about behaviour and describe it will change the language and kinds of targets we are likely to set for short-term and IEP planning:

- A person's behaviour does *not* make that person. We are more than the sum total of observable behaviours.

- Behaviour is the *outward manifestation* (in action or words) of our inner drives (or motivations), our understanding (or construction) of the world around us, our longer-term emotions and immediate feelings, and our general personality characteristics.

- Personal beliefs or more enduring characteristics of our personality that are *learnt* may change slowly or gradually but behaviour can change rapidly in response to both internal and external factors.

It is important to keep these characteristics in mind when formulating and implementing targets, whether they are short-term or more medium-term IEP targets. The short-term targets for the learner should serve the purposes of the longer-term targets and hence give some idea of progression – answering the 'What next?' question.

It is important, at this stage, to be aware that 'managing' behaviour and setting targets is more that just observing and analysing. *Teachers' and other adults' actions, beliefs and attitudes* also play an important part in the whole process. Decisions have to be made and careful discrimination is necessary to separate 'teacher targets' (in managing the behaviour) from 'learner targets' (in learning new behaviours, beliefs, knowledge, understanding or skills, for example). To get these muddled could lead to an adult equating their need to 'manage' a behaviour with an appropriate target for the pupil – they are not the same. For example, a teacher may 'give praise for specific achievements' whereas the pupil is 'learning to recognise his own successes (self-review)' on the path to becoming a more independent learner.

A broader organic and dynamic model

Dilts's *Unified Field* (adapted from O'Connor and Seymour 1990) is a useful model with which to look at behaviour, both our own and that of the pupils we work with. The Unified Field model is elegant in that it proposes that personal change, learning and communication are organic. They do not take place in a fragmentary or fragmented way. Learning and change can take place at different levels. This model is also useful in helping to make decisions about what level it is best to intervene at.

1. **Spiritual (not necessarily religious).** This is the deepest level, where we consider and act out the great metaphysical questions. Why are we here? What is our purpose? The spiritual level guides and shapes our lives, and underpins our existence. Any change at this level has profound repercussions on all other levels.

2. **Identity.** This is my basic sense of self, my core values and mission in life. Children develop this gradually as they go through school. In schools, self-esteem, self-concept and self-image are the important areas for consideration.

3. **Beliefs or constructs.** The various ideas we think are true, and use as a basis for daily action. Beliefs can be both permissions and limitations. Everyone has beliefs or constructs. They form the basis of the way that we *anticipate* events and the behaviour of others in our lives. If we can't anticipate, then life becomes very difficult indeed.

4. **Capability or skill.** These are the groups or sets of behaviours, general skills and strategies that we use in our life to achieve our goals, give us control over the environment or explore new sensations and learn new concepts.

5. **Behaviour.** The specific reactions and actions we carry out, regardless of our capability.

6. **Environment.** What we react to, our surroundings, and other people we meet.

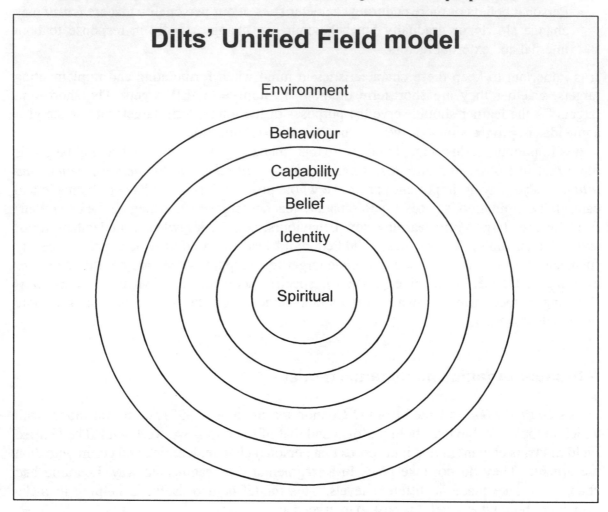

Dilts' Unified Field model

Environment

Behaviour

Capability

Belief

Identity

Spiritual

Figure 6

Do we begin by considering a pupil's behaviour and the events in his or her life – or are we going to look at skills, beliefs or capabilities? Or do we really take them all into account? For teaching purposes, a child is a whole – not a set of behaviours. Robert Dilts further proposes that, 'Change at higher (*more central*) levels will always affect the lower levels . . .'

Looking at Figure 6, we can see that:

● changes in capability or skill will have a greater and more long-lasting effect on behaviours and learning than, say, a change in room temperature;

● human beings function in an organic way so that deeper levels of belief and thought have an influence on behaviour all the time;

● one change in belief can affect a whole range of behaviours;

- whereas it is likely to take a lot of behavioural change to effect one change in belief through positive experience.

A person may change their whole lifestyle because of a change of spiritual nature which affects identity, belief *and lots of behaviours*. Robert Dilts has built this simple, elegant model for thinking about personal change, learning and communication that brings together these ideas of context, relationship, levels of learning and perceptual position. It also forms a context for thinking about the way in which you develop targets for learning. Using this model you can identify the best point to intervene to bring about new learning or make the desired change. Learning and change can take place at different levels.

> Our total personality is like a hologram, a three dimensional image created by beams of light. Any piece of the hologram will give you the whole image. How I behave may change some beliefs about myself. However change in belief will definitely change how I behave. Change at a high level will always affect the lower levels. It will be more pervasive and lasting. So if you want to change behaviour, work with capability of belief. If there is a lack of capability, work with beliefs. Beliefs select capabilities which select behaviours, which in turn directly build on our environment. A supportive environment is imporant, a hostile environment can make any change difficult.
>
> (O'Connor and Seymour 1990)

The target setting, monitoring and evaluation of progress for pupils with EBD should not be limited to a narrow 'behavioural' process but should take place at a level appropriate to the needs and development of the pupil. If we are concerned with skills, then the IEP should reflect clearly the skills we have targeted. If it is understanding, then there should be assessment of existing beliefs and attainment of new concepts through a carefully planned curriculum or developmental framework. If this is not in existence, then it is impossible to measure progress towards anything. 'Progress' becomes a term devalued and limited to one person's conceptual framework – often not shared with the learner. Hence the emphasis in this book away from 'behavioural targets' often constructed as a management tool or simply to get access to the learning environment and towards more educational goals that are *embedded* in a proper curriculum.

The model can equally well be applied to problems. For example, I might misspell a word. I could put this down to the environment; the noise distracted. I could leave it at the level of behaviour; I got this one word wrong. I could generalise and question my capability with words. Or, I could start to believe I need to do more work to improve, or I could call my identity into question by thinking I'm stupid. Behaviour is often taken as evidence of identity or capability, and this is how confidence and competence are destroyed in the classroom. Getting a sum wrong does not mean you are stupid or that you are poor at maths. To think this is to confuse logical levels, equivalent to thinking a 'No Smoking' sign in a cinema applies to the characters in the film.

> Our beliefs strongly influence our behaviour. They motivate us and share what we do. It is difficult to learn anything without believing it will be pleasant and to our advantage . . . Beliefs are the inner map we use to make sense of the world. They give stability and continuity.
>
> (O'Connor and Seymour 1990)

The consequences for IEP planning and implementation lie in the ways in which evaluation is phrased and progress is monitored. Instead of batteries of behavioural targets that are for the benefit of, and individualised to, the learner, should we not develop coherent learning outcomes in spiritual, moral, cultural, personal and social development that form into a curriculum? This is now being done and it will enhance and enrich the whole process of working on IEPs for behaviour and emotional development, placing teaching interventions firmly back into the educational domain.

The personal and social skills 'model'

This way of responding to difficult behaviour is an alternative to the notion of something being inherently wrong with the child which can be reduced or cured by a specific form of treatment (the 'psycho-dynamic' or 'medical model'). It is an *educational (or learning) model'*. It implies that by careful assessment and observation of existing behaviour and social skills, followed by planned intervention through direct teaching *embedded in* a progressive curriculum within a structured social environment, behaviour can be changed *as a learning process*. This makes the pupil into a learner again, not a client, a patient or a problem to 'manage'. Nor a recipient of one-sided contracts or concocted rewards systems or other short-term arrangements – although these may have a place as 'access' strategies.

The 'challenge' is to understand the learned behaviour, the child's motivation and personal world and the context within which s/he operates both at home and at school. It is also to modify our own assumptions in the face of observation and discussion.

One key to success in dealing with challenging behaviours is to take up the notion that 'behaviour' can be changed, as a learning process, and that it is more likely to happen when the problems are carefully described and shared. The discussion should then lead to an *agreed approach* which, having been thoroughly explored before being adopted, can then be *implemented consistently by all concerned*.

The basic need of children

Maslow 1954 propounded a theory that people are motivated by five basic groups of needs, which he called a 'hierarchy of needs'; see Figure 7. The primary need is that of physical survival, and until this need is met people are not able to satisfy needs further up the hierarchy. This is true of each successive stage.

Much of the activity of teaching and learning centres around the higher needs of social, self-esteem and self-realisation. According to Maslow, these can only be achieved when a child has the physiological and safety needs in place. Many children, for a variety of reasons, have not had their basic needs met, particularly in early childhood. The starting point therefore for teaching such children and trying to help them though their difficulties must be to meet, or support arrangements to meet, these basic needs.

A hierarchy of needs (adopted from Maslow 1954)

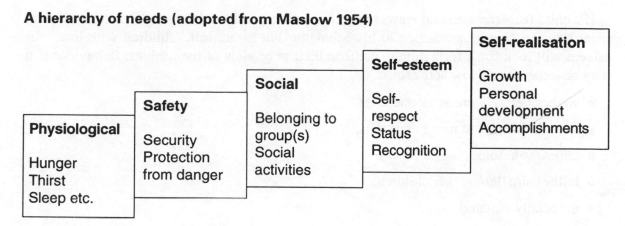

Figure 7

Self-esteem

A full consideration of this aspect of the learner is not appropriate in this book. However, it is worth clarifying the difference between the terms often used in mapping progress and formulating targets for IEPs. The terms below are often used interchangeably but are not the same and will have consequences for the kind of targets that are formulated.

Self-concept

This is an abstract concept, based on a pupil's overall appreciation of his own abilities, feelings and understanding of him of herself and how these interact with each other and with the demands of the world around him or her. To be able to put together a self-concept requires a certain development level or appropriate experiences that lead to the formation of an overall self-concept.

Self-image

A child grows up with all sorts of ideas about himself. These are acquired and influenced by his perception of how he is accepted and valued by significant others e.g. teachers, parents, friends. This self-image goes with him at all times and influences what he does and how he behaves.

Ideal self

From interactions with others, the child forms an impression of the abilities and personal qualities which are admired and valued. A picture of an ideal self is formed.

Self-esteem

This is primarily a measurement of how a child feels about himself. It arises from either a total evaluation a person makes about himself and the degree of respect with which he regards himself or from an intuitive reaction to the actions of others, particularly significant others. High self-esteem provides a child with the confidence to attempt difficult things without fear of failure. A child with a low self-esteem finds it difficult to try new strategies. He protects what he has and continues to behave in a manner consistent with his poor views of himself.

If a child feels rejected and views himself as unacceptable and valueless, then he does not regard disapproval as a reaction to his behaviour but to himself. Children with low self-esteem will look for information to confirm their poor view of themselves. Behaviour that may be indicative of low self-esteem:

- wishes he/she were someone else;
- finds it difficult to make decisions;
- appears anxious;
- bullies smaller/weaker children;
- is socially isolated;
- lacks confidence;
- rarely laughs or smiles;
- gets upset by personal mistakes;
- is rigid in thinking;
- finds it difficult to work independently.

The importance of a good understanding by teachers of self-esteem lies in the formulating of targets. 'Raising self-esteem' is not such a useful target for an IEP, although it may be a laudable long-term aim. Targets for IEPs need to be couched in measurable terms and strategies can then emanate from them. A target for the learner is more likely to have to be – 'able to distinguish between areas where he can succeed and those that he finds difficult'.

Some children and young people have come to believe that achievement and success are not only impossible but completely out of their control. What is more, there is probably a deep-seated belief that they have no influence or impact on what goes on around them or on events in their life. Self-esteem is not a panacea to changing the child. It has less to do with any internal impairment of emotion or personality but more to do with the impact of other people, significant and less significant, and including social exclusion, conditioning and cultural factors. If none of the external factors change, then internal constructs will not change either. A positive school environment may compensate for problems outside school (or a positive home environment may compensate for a negative school environment) but changes may have to be made in both for a person's self-esteem to be raised permanently.

Self-monitoring and self-control

'Self control' refers to a broad range of skills which enables the individual to monitor and direct his/her own behaviour. This includes the skills required to tackle and solve new problems as well as those being required to deploy behaviours already in the individual's repertoire. The concept includes the skills themselves and the direction given by the individual as opposed to some external source.

(Clements 1987)

The capacity for self-direction, or at least reaching the maximum possible level of self-direction for each individual pupil, is fundamental to education and behaviour programmes.

The society we live in regards the capacity of self-direction as important and it is therefore linked to status that a young adult will achieve after school. In addition to this, it is very difficult to get any individual to 'generalise' or maintain any behaviour changes (that may have been 'managed') unless they are able to self-direct and problem solve.

Four main ways in which 'self-control' can be developed

- It is intimately related to the development of language and its direct role over behaviour in general. *Internal language* is used to reflect upon and guide the child's own behaviours. It is thus related to the quality of daily communication that the child experiences and the models of language supplied by the teacher or other adults. An example is talking yourself down when overexcited – expressing your feelings and thus helping to manage them.

- *Self-management* provides the pupil with *meaningful 'cues' for appropriate behaviour* but cues which the pupil retains under his/her own control. For example, cues or questions to promote appropriate social behaviours – 'Now what we do when . . .?' or a particular look.

- The *teaching analysis of social situations*, self-awareness, empathy, self-instruction, self-monitoring, relaxation and appropriate assertiveness skills: an example of this is 'anger management'. Usually used with adults but may have relevance, in parts, to younger persons.

- *Self-advocacy* is a means by which the individual will effect change towards a desired goal by their own efforts. It aims to develop the ability to analyse problems, make simple decisions and act effectively (and appropriately) to implement those decisions.

Involving the learner: Institutional self-review

Regular schools with this inclusive orientation are the most effective means of combating discriminatory attitudes, creating welcoming communities, building an inclusive society and achieving education for all; moreover, they provide an effective education to the majority of children and improve the efficiency and ultimately the cost-effectiveness of the entire education system.

(UNESCO Salamanca Statement 1989)

How do practices in the school impact upon the individual pupil with EBD?

- Pupils are not passive receivers of information. *They have to participate in their own learning.* Pupils should be given every opportunity to take responsibility and to make a full contribution to improving behaviour in schools. The active participation of pupils in shaping and reviewing the school's behaviour policy should be encouraged, in order to foster a sense of collective responsibility.

- *Records of Achievement* and work experience are both ways of improving the motivation of disaffected pupils. Schools, LEAs and employers should increase their cooperation in developing means of increasing pupils' motivation, such as in compacts between these bodies.

- *Certain pupils are more likely to present behaviour or attendance problems than others.* In the case of attendance, the pupil most at risk seems to be the low achiever from a severely disadvantaged background. In the case of severely disruptive behaviour, however, the picture is less clear in terms of material circumstances such as housing and family income. Boys are about four times more likely than girls to be involved. Pupils who show severely disruptive behaviour are likely to be rated as below average ability by their teachers and to have a history of low achievement at school. They are also likely to come from highly stressed family backgrounds.

- *Such 'risk profiles' must be treated with caution. The Elton Report 1987 emphasises the importance of teachers' expectations and of low expectation leading to self-fulfilling prophecies.* It is crucial for teachers to be wary of stereotypes. However, while 'risk profiles' are dangerous tools, they can help to sharpen teachers' awareness of potential problems and to present the possibility for remedial action before behaviour patterns are set. Pupil records should thus cover their pastoral as well as their learning needs.

- A small minority of pupils have such *severe and persistent behaviour problems* as a result of emotional, psychological or neurological disturbances that their needs cannot be met in mainstream schools. *Such pupils will require a statement of special educational need.* The role of educational psychologists is central to such assessment and statementing.

- Other pupils with special educational needs may have *behaviour problems as a result of the frustration caused by their learning difficulties.* Such learning difficulties may not always be recognised because teachers have explained lack of progress in terms of laziness or bad behaviour rather than learning difficulties.

The UN Convention on the Rights of the Child (1989)

Article 12 states the right of the child to express an opinion and to have that opinion taken into account, in any matter or procedure affecting the child.

Article 29 states that a child's education should be directed at developing the child's personality and talents, and mental and physical abilities to their fullest potential. It also states that education shall prepare the child for an active and responsible life as an adult, fostering respect for basic human rights and developing respect for the child's own cultural and national values and those of others.

Involving the learner: Ideas for action

'Challenging' is a blanket generalisation to describe difficult behaviour, with the implication that it challenges our personal resources in dealing with it. Unfortunately. all these labels – disturbed, challenging, difficult, bad, etc. – say more about the adult's problem in dealing with, and the adult's feelings about, a particular child's behaviour than anything useful about the behaviour itself. It is important when writing targets and evaluating progress that a child is not measured in terms of how the teacher (or other adult) feels about the situation. In order for the daily record keeping and assessment to be useful in refining and developing IEP targets, it must be focused and the comments must be based on *progress* against curriculum, personal, social, spiritual, moral or other educational targets.

Make up your own mind about these comments in the following tables. Do they tell you something specific about *progress* against a developmental continuum or are they isolated comments?

	'Behaviour' or learning targets (samples from record keeping)	**Evaluative comments (are they?)** (daily logs, behaviour reports, IEPs)
1	Encourage ___ to socialise with his peers	Spent time on playground with ___
2	Will sit still in class for 10 minutes	Got up when Mr ___ came in
3	Greet his peers in a friendly manner	Achieved SSC Target 10, Level 2
4	Reduce the number of angry outbursts	Behaved well and was amenable
5	Ask for help when needed	Confidently asked three times in English lesson for the words
6	Doesn't understand stealing is wrong	Must be accompanied by adult in the shop
7	Understanding 'Stress' Part 1 . . . by recognising the signs of stress	Unit assessment KS 4 Scheme PSE 'Life Skills' – achieved level C 'pass'
8	'Helping ourselves' – switching on the computer – using mouse to select icon	IT (working towards) KS1 Level 1a – still not discriminating between icons
9	Will address teachers appropriately when given instructions	Was polite to Mr ___ today

To be worthwhile, the targets and their *evaluative comments have to lead somewhere* for that pupil. Can you see where any of the above comments are leading? If the comments do not lead anywhere or are not *embedded in a larger continuum or framework*, such as a curriculum, then progress is measured in very limited, subjective terms. Also, the *evaluative comment must be focused on the original targets*, otherwise we are not evaluating progress but something completely different. From the above examples:

1. 'Encourage __ to socialise with his peers' is a vague target for the learner and may not mean much to him anyway – so *it is a teacher target, not a learner target*. 'Spent time on playground with __' is a description of what happened, not an evaluation of progress.

2. This comment has nothing to do with the original target, probably because the expectation is not planned into the lesson or activity.

3. 'Greet his peers in a friendly manner' may seem like a vague target but it is *given precise focus by its place on a planned continuum (curriculum or developmental framework)*. The evaluative comment is a reference to the Social Skills Curriculum attainment target at the appropriate level.

6. This *is not a target at all* – it is an assessment of the child's understanding based on whatever evidence might have been available (possibly on an incident or behaviour observed). The evaluative comment *is not an evaluative comment* at all – it is a management strategy for the adults (i.e. it is an adult or teacher target, not a pupil's target). *It has no place on a child's IEP or weekly/daily plan* but on a management plan for the adults in terms of 'procedures'.

Now look at 4, 5, 7, 8 and 9. Comment or discuss with colleagues.

- Do you think the targets are good? Relevant and meaningful part of a meaningful progression?

- Are they targets you can make evaluative comments about or measure progress in any way?

- Do the comments truly give a picture of *progress* for that child?

- Are they evaluative in any way?

- Are they part and parcel of an existing scheme or curriculum – cutting down on extra paperwork?

Parental involvement: Principles

How can parents be involved in IEPs?

The relationships between parents of children with special educational needs and the school which their child is attending has a crucial bearing on the child's educational progress and the effectiveness of any school based action.

Most schools already have effective working relationships with parents, including the parents of children with special educational needs.

School based arrangements should ensure that assessment reflects a sound and comprehensive knowledge of a child and his or her responses to a variety of carefully planned and recorded actions which take account of the wishes, feelings and knowledge of parents at all stages.

Children's progress will be diminished if their parents are not seen as partners in the educational process with unique knowledge and information to impart.

Professional help can seldom be wholly effective unless it builds upon parents' capacity to be involved and unless professionals take account of what they say and treat their views and anxieties as intrinsically important.

- Parental involvement within a child's IEP is vital. It is not an intrusion into a school's response to special needs nor can it become an afterthought once procedures are put in place.

- Parents have a right to be informed about and involved in the decision-making process regarding their child. The insights and opinions of parents are at least as valid as those of professionals involved within the IEP.

- The relationship that a parent of a child with special needs has with the school will be an extension and elaboration of existing good policy and practice for parental partnership with the school.

- Having a child with any special educational need may cause extra stress and worry as well as imposing additional responsibilities on the parent.

(Code of Practice 2:28)

Why are some parents reluctant to participate with their child's IEP?

Parents of pupils with EBD may experience difficulty in working collaboratively with school staff on their child's IEP because:

- They may feel that 'behaviour' and 'happiness' are very much their responsibility – more than, say, helping their child with academic work. Basically, they feel it is 'their fault' and that the school is judgemental and/or critical in its approach.

- They may themselves have experienced similar difficulties to those being experienced by their child and are aware of the effect they had on their own future in terms of achievement, earnings, relationships, health and personal happiness. Like their child, they may be 'fearing failure' and fearing the future.

- They may have had less than happy experiences at school and not feel comfortable in school settings.

- They may themselves be experiencing difficulties and conditions which prevent them from being able to contribute to the planning and provision involved in their child's IEP. This in turn adds to the guilt and helplessness they experience.

- They may not know 'how' to help their child but not have the confidence to ask for assistance.

- The home situation often does not afford the structure and predictability needed to effect a behaviour change. Emotional involvement inevitable between parents and their offspring may adversely affect the consistency with which strategies can be applied. Home provides the 'personalised, social, unstructured' setting conditions in which EBD children may find it particularly difficult to develop and exhibit 'new behaviours'.

- The home situations may be rich in 'cues' or 'triggers' for disputes (e.g. siblings). Expected behaviour at home may be very different from that expected at school.

- The child may find it 'easier' to manipulate the system at home by playing one parent off against another. Schools may find it easier to 'agree' boundaries.

- Some parents may find getting to school and attending meetings difficult.

Parental involvement: Institutional self-review

How can IEP planning address these concerns?

- The Individual Education Plan is a document. It has a structure, 'boxes' that have to be filled in and as such is 'impersonal'. *Parents, particularly those who are themselves anxious, may find it easier to work with staff concerned on a focused impersonal task* than engage in a discussion about 'the behaviour of your child'.

- The IEP provides a *focus* for collaborative planning; filling in the plan enables 'joint attention' with parents to be established at an early point in the meeting.

- The *data gathering procedure is not intrusive* and is directed towards provision, not towards apportioning blame.

- The parents are asked to state what worries them about their child ('concerns'). This *'concern' focus allows parents to give their perspective initially* rather than adopting a defensive role.

- 'Agreeing targets' does provide a framework for collaborative working. Some SENCOs have suggested that *if three targets are to be selected, then at least one should be chosen by the parents.*

- Parents are in a unique position to suggest which strategies would work for their child. This places them in an *appropriate position as provider of information* to support school planning, rather than receivers of 'what we are going to do . . .'.

- The fact that the IEP is a 'planning' and not a reporting document affords the opportunity for the SENCO/CT/outside agencies *to suggest to parents what strategies might be used for meeting targets*. The specific advice central to IEP planning can be very useful to parents who only have their own experiences and strategies to fall back on.

- The need to review IEPs on a regular basis means that *parents can be kept informed* as part of an ongoing process – not on a 'crisis' basis. This built-in support can be particularly valuable to parents of an EBD child who may have only had support at times when things were not going well. This gives a mechanism for supporting parents before total breakdown.

- The need to record 'pupil strengths' on the IEP *allows parents to direct attention towards positive behaviours* rather than reporting difficulties.

- The IEP provides *an opportunity for parents to work with their child on agreed targets*. This is in contrast to plans which involve adults 'talking about' the child and making plans 'for' and not 'with' them.

- SEN pupils are often subjected to many 'assessments' and advice. Parents can become confused by this. As *effort by all concerned in the IEP is focused towards the development and achievement of targets,* this can result in parents receiving more coordinated support than they might normally experience.

The mother of nine-year-old **Shane Powell** who has been expelled for kicking his Headteacher said the trouble started when classmates bullied him because of his disabilities. The Headmaster said he regretted having to expel Shane but had no alternative. It was the first time he had been hit in 23 years at school. **Wiltshire County Council** is trying to find another school for Shane and meanwhile has offered home tuition.

(*Western Daily Press* 13 May 1996)

Formulating targets in the context of out of school influences

Outside influences affect the nature of the targets and more importantly their chances of success. To completely ignore the *outside influences* and concentrate upon 'in-school' effects is both a solution and a problem at the same time.

- They may continually frustrate progress in school or reverse gains made.

- They may be marshalled to help with in-school targets, given the right conditions.

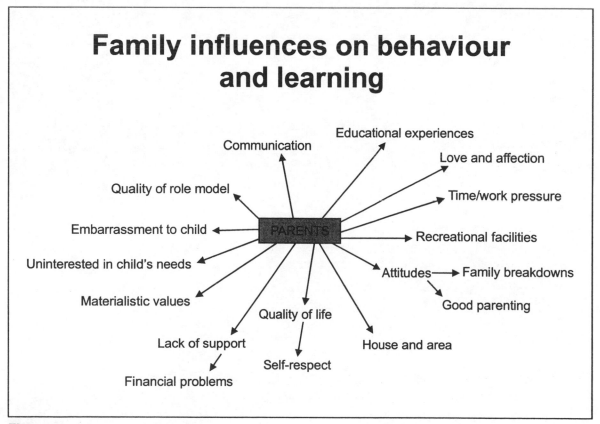

Figure 8

This leaves a dilemma in relation to setting targets and the strategies that emanate from them. If the strategy involves factors that may well cause it to fail and these are beyond the teacher's control, do you leave out the target altogether? Or, do you think again and try to construct a target that is less desirable but more likely to be achieved in school?

A number of teachers were asked what factors in families have a significant impact on behaviour and learning.

- How might the achieving of IEP targets be affected by any one or more of the factors in Figure 8?

- What effect would this have on your IEP and its targets?

For example, a typical IEP target might be 'responds to requests'. If communication at home is not good, the pupil might be accused, by parents, of not taking any notice when, in fact, instructions are rarely made clear. The pupil might have got into the habit of ignoring requests because they are confusing.

Parental involvement: Ideas for action

The table below is nothing more than a tentative suggestion. It is not possible to have 'parent targets' in the true sense, unless there is sufficient time to engage in a development with parents involving much discussion. However, it does serve to illustrate the fact that it is necessary to decide who does what and what is really a useful *pupil target* and one that could be sensibly included on an IEP. Try some for yourself.

Types of target

Observations or sources of problem	Teacher target? In-school change	Parent target? Marshalling support	Suitable IEP target? Pupil target
Family interaction is negative – picking out failure regularly for the child. Little encouragement.	Find success for the pupil when possible – encourage independent self-review by pupil.	Talk about child's achievements and encourage parents to do so.	Is able to recognise his own good work. Sets achievable criteria for success and celebrates it.
Role models/TV encourage aggression.	Develop critical analysis of TV in curriculum.	Discuss TV watching habits and their result in school.	Pupil learns to discriminate fact from fantasy.
Social boundaries are very different from the school's.			
Peer pressure leads child into trouble.			
Culture/racism/ religion – pupil is subject to some form of bullying.			
Unemployment in the family causes many rows.			
??			

Training and continuing professional development: Principles

Summary

- There should be a constant review of training initiatives, both in Initial Teacher Training (ITT) and in Continuing Professional Development (CPD), in the basic qualities of good teaching, managing a classroom and forming positive relationships. These are the conditions that will reduce potential disaffection and disruption to a minimum.

- Continuing professional development should also include: pupil management skills; early years identification of EBD; incorporating language and literacy into programmes for EBD pupils; and continuing detailed training in matching education to particular individual needs.

- Teachers and other staff need substantial training in order to be able to separate straightforward 'naughtiness' or slightly divergent behaviour from behaviour that stems from a genuine underlying problem.

- All staff should have training in observing pupils' responses accurately and sensitively and in making objective evaluative comments to record their observations.

- All staff need continuing training in contributing to the team or joint effort – training in teamwork skills to implement IEPs.

- Appropriate staff with monitoring or coordinating responsibilities will need training in the organisational skills of monitoring and coordination to ensure the quality of provision and planning.

- Children need to feel they are learning, and feedback from teachers which is focused and sustaining will also motivate and enhance pupils' self-esteem. Training for enhanced interpersonal skills as well as classroom management is important.

Pupils with emotional and/or behavioural difficulties have learning difficulties as defined at paragraph 2:1 of the Code of Practice. They may fail to meet expectations in school and in some, but by no means all, cases may also disrupt the education of others.

Emotional and behavioural difficulties may result, for example, from: abuse or neglect; physical or mental illness; sensory or physical impairment; or psychological trauma. In some cases, emotional and behavioural difficulties may arise from, or be exacerbated by, circumstances within the school environment. They may also be associated with other learning difficulties. The causes and effects of EBD are discussed in more detail in the DES 1990 circular *The Education of Children with Emotional and Behavioural Difficulties*, where the concept of a continuum of difficulty is developed.

| | Considered judgements – not facts | | |
Description or observation	Clear source(s) of evidence or detail	Are there contextual or reactive factors?	Are there indeterminate or internal factors?	Comment on degree to which it affects learning
The child is unusually withdrawn, lacks confidence	Classroom observations – CA + teacher. Parents have commented too.	Yes – occurs more often when child is asked to read but other times too.	Don't know – further observation and consultations required.	Hampers reading because of avoidance – and relationships with peers and adults.
Severely impaired social interaction or communication	In the classroom – gets agitated very quickly – can't ask for help when needed – finds it hard to start and finish a conversation – or follow two requests.	Not subject to teasing – over-reacts to small changes or well meant comments from peers.	Has some unconscious movements or small 'tics' – needs further consultations.	Ability to express himself orally is poor but enjoys repetitive written tasks – finds it hard to move from one activity to the next.
. . . and so on . . .				

The following examples need further consideration before judgements are made. Perhaps you have similar examples to try and work through in the boxes above?

- evidence of a significantly restricted repertoire of activities, interests and imaginative development;

- the child attends school irregularly;

- evidence of any obsessions, particularly with eating habits;

- evidence of any substance or alcohol misuse;

- child displays unpredictable, bizarre, obsessive, violent or severely disruptive behaviour;

- the child has participated in or has been subject to bullying at school;

- has been subject to neglect and/or abuse at home; and/or has faced major difficulties at home;

- any suggestion that the child may have a significant mental or physical health problem;

- any sudden unpredictable changes in the child's behaviour which have no obvious cause, but which might include a developing neurological impairment, epilepsy, or another physical cause.

. . . there is a significant discrepancy between, on the one hand, the child's cognitive ability and expectations of the child as assessed by his or her teachers, parents and others directly concerned, supported, as appropriate, by appropriately administered standardised tests and, on the other hand, the child's academic attainment as measured by National Curriculum assessments and teachers' own recorded assessments of the child's classroom work, including any portfolio of the child's work compiled to illustrate his or her progress.

(Code of Practice)

Training and continuing professional development: Institutional self-review

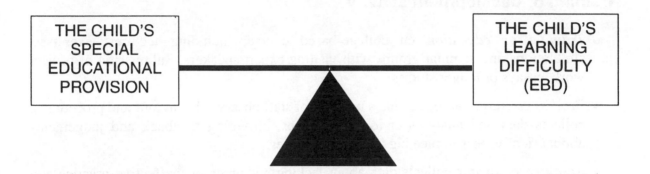

| THE CHILD'S SPECIAL EDUCATIONAL PROVISION | THE CHILD'S LEARNING DIFFICULTY (EBD) |

There are a number of actions the school should take care to follow. These include:

- *seeking appropriate external advice* and then, following thorough discussions with the child, *formulating, implementing, monitoring and evaluating individual education plans*, including a behaviour management programme;

- following, as appropriate in the individual case, *the provisions of its policies on behaviour and on pastoral care and guidance*;

- *fully informing all staff* of the child's difficulties and maintaining a consistent approach to remedying these difficulties across the school;

- seeking a *constructive relationship with the child's parents/carers*, encouraging them to participate in their child's education, including visiting the school on a regular basis;

- where appropriate, *notifying and seeking the involvement of the education welfare service and/or the social services department*;

- *securing access for the child to appropriate information technology* as a means of motivating and stimulating the child, for example word processing facilities, painting programs and other software which encourages communication and self-expression, providing training in the use of that technology across the curriculum in school, and wherever appropriate, at home;

- with the parents' consent, notifying and seeking the assistance of the school doctor and/or the child's general practitioner, as appropriate.

(Extracted from Code of Practice)

Training and continuing professional development: Ideas for action

Training or development activity

- *Training or education* on college-based course, including lectures, exercises, simulations and seminar groups with visiting expert speakers. Submission of project work, essays or longer studies.

- *Process consultation* means that a member of staff observes behaviour and procedures, collects data and analyses ongoing processes, providing feedback and judgements about effectiveness in meeting its own objectives.

- *Resource innovato*r collects data about lacking resources or ineffective practice and then, through analysis of the 'need', links with or makes/develops the appropriate resources and also evaluates these.

- *Agent of change* sometimes engenders confrontation and insecurity but is interested in the people and events that enable improvements to take place. Sometimes brings together new combinations of people and resources, followed by systematic collection of information which is reported back to the organisation. This deals with planning and goal setting.

- *Organisation development task forces* (sometimes called 'Working Parties'). Ad hoc and delegated or chosen groups set up to provide structure for solving problems, engaging development work and carrying out plans. Focusing on structural factors, work flow systems, and means of accomplishing tasks.

Generating a view of training needs

This is not a simple matter and it could be said that *all of the training undertaken in a school*, whether it is to develop security in subject knowledge or to understand more about self-esteem, will have an impact on the education of pupils experiencing EBD. The table below suggests some examples of specific areas for review. It is not exhaustive and experiences will suggest many more. Each box could have many more components but often these will be specific to a school's needs.

	Individual IEPs – involving class teaching, subjects, lessons		Group assimilation of collective IEPs		
	Teacher	CA/LSA	SMT	Governors	SENCO
Assess: Strengths and concerns	Consistent use of baselines. Recognising when learning has taken place and success.	Questions to assess understanding. Planning to observe and record. Structuring situations for assessment and recording.	Resources available. Staff cohesion and knowledge. Audit of SEN generally and match of provision to levels of need.		*Some* careful use of diagnostic tests. A variety of assessment methods – support to teachers and CAs.
Formulate: Targets and goals	Goal setting. SMART plans. Including parents.	Understand precise learning objectives.	Review of school development plan.		Co-teaching and collaborative skills.
Design: Strategies for access and for learning	Circle time, positive behaviour management, PSE, teaching SMSC curriculum	Interpreting observations and pupil responses. Develop answers to questions	Whole-school approaches are working – any parts need development?		Consultation and advisory skills.
Monitor: Ongoing progress	Records and lesson planning. Relationship to schemes of work.	What do pupil's answers and responses tell me?	Focusing meetings on EBD issues. Involving parents successfully.	Is the school coordinating educational effort efficiently?	Liaison with teachers and CAs. Expectations for progress – matched to outcomes.
Evaluate: Progress and impact on learning or access	Academic progress. Personal and social curriculum – is it effective?	Comparing strategies used and their effectiveness.	Relate to school policies (e.g. behaviour and pastoral care, SEN and curriculum). Effectiveness of staffing and collaboration arrangements	Is there efficient use of resources in implementing school policies – SEN, behaviour, pastoral, curriculum and assess-ment?	Match of staff, subjects, activities and learning outcomes to individual needs. Use IEPs to recognise 'group' effects and individual progress.

'Nobody forgets a good teacher', says the Teacher Training Agency (TTA) marketing slogan. There is some truth in this but what is even more apparent in the area of EBD is that 'nothing settles disaffected and disruptive pupils like good teaching'. In terms of formulating and evaluating IEPs, it is necessary to start from an objective baseline assessment. This is not possible unless the conditions in the classroom for most pupils are settled and secure. If disruption is caused by a significant proportion of the class, then it is more likely to be a result of poor teaching, inadequate planning or poor resources and irrelevant or meaningless tasks and activities. If, on the other hand, disruption or challenging behaviour is exhibited by only one, perhaps two pupils in a class, then it is likely that the class is reasonably well organised for most pupils. The two pupils who are disruptive probably need further consideration to get at the causes for the difficulties. Good teaching provides a stable base from which the additional or extra strategies for individuals can be implemented more effectively. Poor teaching only serves to mask any learning or behavioural difficulties by generating poor behaviour in the majority of pupils.

The following checklist lays out elements of effective practice in the classroom to support the formulation and implementation of IEPs that will have some impact upon the problems of an individual child in accessing and responding to the curriculum. Managing and working in a classroom is a complex, interactive and dynamic process requiring considerable, but not superhuman, skills applied with planning and forethought. The following table is essentially a checklist which summarises some of the interactive activities and processes taking place in the classroom. They are all interlinked and should not be seen as separate activities, but for the purposes of analysis they need to be evaluated separately.

Use this checklist to review your own training needs related to developing relationships, classroom management and engaging in effective teaching (including implementing IEPs). These are basic parameters of good group and classroom work. Research and experience have shown conclusively that these alone can reduce to a minimum the potential for disaffection and disruption and that often pupils' behaviour is blamed for outcomes that are a result of disaffection with poor or unsatisfactory teaching. It is understood that all of us have days where we succeed better than other days or off-days from time to time. This is in contrast to a situation where children are regularly disaffected and disruptive because they have got into poor work habits and inconsistent or non-existent routines.

Classroom dynamics

Your review notes Outline skills and understanding you need for:	Areas of activity	Specific points of contact, understanding, knowledge related to the 'Community of the Classroom'
Curriculum and teaching	The quality of pupil's experiences and responses	• The quality of relationships in the classroom is good (pupil:pupil and adults:pupils); • levels of concentration and application are satisfactory; • fostering independent learning skills; • cooperation and collaboration with each other and adults present; • expectations and willingness to take responsibility (for learning); • attitude and interest in the work set.
	Programmes of learning, schemes of work and lesson planning	• Relevant and meaningful activities that motivate and challenge are planned in advance; • expectations are realistic but challenge pupils to move on or to establish good work routines; • there are clear curriculum objectives as well as related individual targets, where appropriate; • the teacher or LSA/SSA has a secure knowledge of the subject or skill/objective being taught; • there are planned activities to reinforce concepts for different levels of attainment (including extension activities for those who need them); • the ideas of extension and reinforcement are developed through the setting of homework, whenever possible.
	Monitoring pupil's progress	• Awareness of comparison with national expected levels of attainment (NC); • reference to cross-curricular elements and skills of oracy, literacy, numeracy and IT; • assess pupil's progress regularly during the lesson and give (positive/constructive) feedback;

Your review notes Outline skills and understanding you need for:	Areas of activity	Specific points of contact, understanding, knowledge related to the 'Community of the Classroom'
		• marking of work or other reinforcing strategies are used sensitively and effectively; • are all pupils making the progress that is expected of them at their own level? • there is purposeful and useful recording of progress in curriculum subjects and personal development.
	The use of human and material resources	• Due attention is paid to the health and safety of all in the classroom (including dealing with outbursts); • materials and aids or technology enable pupils to present their work as well as possible and take pride in it; • the deployment of learning support personnel and volunteers is targeted to achieving the group or individual learning objectives; • IT is used (including video and other means) to make the lessons more accessible and interesting (and they work!).
Team work	Roles and room management	• The roles of all personnel in the classroom are clearly defined (e.g. one person teaching a group – one doing individual work/support); • the roles are dynamic and change regularly to suit the purpose of the particular lesson; • actions are planned or thought out and agreed between the personnel in the class; • pupils also take part in the process of room management (e.g. looking after resources, tidying up, categorising and labelling for storage).
	Subject security and consistency of approach	• Good collaboration between staff enables cohesion and consistency (including subject specialists);

Your review notes Outline skills and understanding you need for:	Areas of activity	Specific points of contact, understanding, knowledge related to the 'Community of the Classroom'
		• recording systems, including pastoral and personal, or social development, are consistent across classes and lessons; • SENCO coordinates effectively.
	Partnership with parents	• Parents regarded as part of the solution, not part of the problem; • information is shared through a systematic approach (to IEPs?); • school ethos welcomes parents' interest; • careful planning of homework; • sensitive planning of meetings and systematic contact.
	Other staff in school, multiagency support and approaches	• Planning includes other sources of information and support, as available; • SENCO or key worker has proactive approach to involving other personnel or outside professional help.
Group dynamics	Flexibility of approach	• Teaching skills encompass a variety of presentation approaches and methods; • good planning allows for some individual diversions without losing the flow and focus of the lesson.
	Disruptive behaviours	• Adults have good knowledge of individual pupils and their backgrounds, learning needs and predisposition; • there are planned proactive responses readily available to deal with disruption (whole-school as well as class).
	1:1 opportunities	• Planning recognises the need for systematic individual targets – whether in 1:1 teaching or as part of a group; • spontaneous opportunities outside the classroom are taken to support good learning habits in the classroom;

Your review notes Outline skills and understanding you need for:	Areas of activity	Specific points of contact, understanding, knowledge related to the 'Community of the Classroom'
		● individual or special rewards given for personal endeavour as well as academic attainment.
	Groupings and group work	● Teaching involves some organised movement around the class during the day; ● social groupings are acknowledged sometimes alongside more formal academic groups or sets; ● no groups are identified as the failures or bottom set; ● pupils who are disruptive or have special learning needs are not consistently grouped together.
	Layout of room and resources	● Resources that are in constant use are clearly labelled and accessible; ● pupils' workbooks and equipment are placed or organised to be available with minimum disruption; ● layout of tables and chairs reduces negative contacts among pupils and facilitates attention to the task(s) at hand.
Resources	Curriculum materials	● These are chosen to fit the task and provide adequate interest or stimulation to pupils; ● the level of cross-curricular skills (e.g. literacy, numeracy etc.) required to understand them matches pupils' abilities; ● they are multi-sensory and differentiated for individual needs where appropriate.
	Planning and acquisition	● The use of IT and other technological resources meets the requirements of the task; ● planning for use of resources is creative and explores some new approaches (e.g. not 'death by worksheet').
	Spaces and organisation	● Spaces are used effectively to foster independent learning in the classroom and other spaces;

Your review notes Outline skills and understanding you need for:	Areas of activity	Specific points of contact, understanding, knowledge related to the 'Community of the Classroom'
		• the organisation of resources and their use allows pupils to take responsibility for them, where possible.
Time management	Teaching sessions/units	• These are clearly planned to have a purpose and an end result, if not then a specific process; • they are realistic and appropriate in length for the ages and abilities of the class; • the adults present are available for feedback, comment or support of one kind or another, at regular intervals.
	Planning and communication	• Sufficient time is planned and available in the school for proper planning and communication (e.g. across the subjects); • lessons are planned to allow time for introduction/orientation at the beginning and review or (self-)evaluation at the end.
	Beginnings and ends	• Teaching sessions have clear beginnings and ends so that pupils can learn routines; • expectations and explanations about what is going to happen are clear at the start; • pupils can understand at the beginning the sequence of events that is about to take place; • there are frequent checks through the lesson to comment on progress, behaviour, organisation etc.; • at the end of the lesson, time is allowed for review and (self-)evaluation by adults and pupils and for any questions or misunderstandings to be cleared up.

Effective teaching, classroom management and the generation of positive and supportive relationships are key factors in reducing the impact of any pupil's EBD on other pupils and in ensuring a firm foundation on which to formulate, implement and evaluate the school's IEPs.

Bibliography

Argyle, M. (1967) *The Psychology of Inter-Personal Behaviour*. Harmondsworth: Penguin.

Bate, C. and Moss, J. (1997) 'Towards a Behaviour Curriculum', *Educational Psychology in Practice* **13**(3), 176–180.

Blamires, M. (1998) *Implementing Effective Practice for IEPs*. London: David Fulton Publishers.

Bond, T. (1990) *Games for Social Skills*. London: Hutchinson.

Borba, M. and Borba, C. (1978) *Self-Esteem: A Classroom Affair*. London: Harper & Row.

Borba, M. and Borba, C. (1982) *Self-Esteem: A Classroom Affair. Vol. 2*. London: Harper & Row (1996).

Bowers, T. (1996) 'The Trouble with Individual Education Plans', *Managing Schools Today* **5**(5), 13–15.

Bromfield, C. (1992) The Effectiveness of Circle Time as a Strategy for Use in Primary Schools with Special Regard to Children Having Behaviour Problems. University of Plymouth: unpublished M.Ed. (SEN) dissertation.

Canfield, J. and Wells, M. C. (1976) *100 Ways to Enhance Self-Esteem in the Classroom*. London: Prentice-Hall.

Clements, J. (1987) *Severe Learning Difficulties and Psychological Handicap*. Chichester: J. Wiley & Sons.

Cooper, P., Smith, C. J. and Upton, G. (1994) *Emotional and Behavioural Difficulties: Theory to Practice*. London: Routledge.

Cresson, E. (1996) Presentation of the European *Year of Lifelong Learning*. Edinburgh, 22 February. Ref.: SPEECH/96/47.

Curry, M. and Bromfield, C. (1994) *Personal and Social Education for Primary Schools through Circle Time*. Stafford: NASEN Enterprises.

Department for Education (1993) *The Education Act*. London: HMSO.

Department for Education (1994) *Code of Practice: The Identification and Assessment of Special Educational Needs*. London: HMSO: EDUC JO22465NJ 5/94.

Department for Education and Employment (1997) *Green Paper: Excellence for All Children: Meeting Special Educational Needs*. London: HMSO.

Department for Education and Science (1990) *The Education of Children with Emotional and Behavioural Difficulties*. London: HMSO.

Dilts, R. (1983) *Applications of Neuro-Linguistic Programming*. Santa Cruz, CA: Meta Publications.

East Kent Health Promotion Service (1997) *Health Promoting Schools Award*. Canterbury: East Kent Health Promotion Service.

The Elton Report (1987) *Discipline in Schools: Report of the Committee of Enquiry*. London: HMSO.

Feuerstein, R. (1969) *The Instrumental Enrichment Method: An Outline of Theory and Technique*. Jerusalem: HWCRI.

Gary, P. and Noakes, J. (1990) 'Time to Stop Taking the Easy Option'. *Times Educational Supplement*.

Jennings, S. (1992) *Drama Therapy: Theory and Practice 2*. London: Routledge.

Lawrence, D. (1988) *Enhancing Self-Esteem in the Classroom*. London: Paul Chapman.

Lecky, P. (1945) *Self Consistency*. New York: Island Press.

Lloyd, S. R. and Berthelot, C. (1992) *Self-Empowerment: How to Get What You Want from Life*. London: Kogan Page.

MacLeod, D. (1992) 'The rising number of pupils barred from school for bad behaviour is causing alarm bells among parents, teachers and authorities'. *The Independent: Education* 19, Thursday 23 January.

Maslow, A. H. (1954) *Motivation and Personality* (2nd edn.). New York: Harper & Rowe.

McCarthy, D. and Davies, J. (1996) "SEN Resource Pack for Schools". Ilford: Specialist Matters.

McGuiness, J. (1993) *Teachers, Pupils and Behaviour: A Managerial Approach*. London: Cassell.

McNamara, S and Moreton, G. (1995) *Changing Behaviour: Teaching Children with Emotional and Behavioural Difficulties in Primary and Secondary Classrooms*. London: David Fulton Publishers.

O'Connor and Seymour (1990). *Introducing Neuro Linguistic Programming: The New Psychology of Personal Excellence*. London: Mandala Press.

OFSTED (1993) *Handbook for the Inspection of Schools*. London: HMSO.

OFSTED (1995a) *The OFSTED Framework*. London: HMSO.

OFSTED (1995b) *The OFSTED Handbook 10/95*. London: HMSO.

OFSTED (1995c) *Guidance on the Inspection of Nursery and Primary Schools*. London: HMSO.

OFSTED (1995d) *Guidance on the Inspection of Secondary Schools*. London: HMSO.

OFSTED (1995e) *Guidance on the Inspection of Special Schools*. London: HMSO.

OFSTED (1996) *The Implementation of the Code of Practice for Pupils with Special Educational Needs*. London: HMSO.

OFSTED (1996/97) *The SEN Code – 2 Years On*. London: HMSO.

Palmer, P. (1977) *Liking Myself*.   :Impact Publishers.

Parsons, C. *et al*. (1997) *Excluding Primary School Children*. London: Family Policy Studies Centre.

Qualifications and Curriculum Authority (1997) The promotion of pupils' spiritual, moral, social and cultural development: Draft Guidance for pilot work.

Schools' Curriculum and Assessment Authority (1995) *Planning the Curriculum*. London: SCAA.

SENJIT (1995) *Schools Policy Pack*. London: National Children's Bureau.

Thacker, J. (1984) 'Project on Developmental Group Work in Pastoral Care and Personal/Social Education in Junior and Middle Schools'. Report of the First Year of the Project. University of Exeter: Centre for Personal, Social and Moral Education, School of Education.

Topping, K. (1988) *The Peer Tutoring Handbook: Promoting Co-operative Learning*. London: Croom Helm.

UNESCO (1989) *The Salamanca Statement and Framework for Action on Special Needs Education*. Paris: UNESCO.

UNICEF (1989) *The UN Convention on the Rights of the Child*. London: UNICEF.

Warnock, M. (1977) *Report of the Committee of Enquiry into the Education of Handicapped Children and Young People*. London: HMSO.

White, R., Carr, P. and Lowe, N. (1990) *A Guide to the Children Act 1989*. London: